A PRIMER

OF

SPOKEN ENGLISH

A PRIMER
OF
SPOKEN ENGLISH

HENRY SWEET

GYAN

Published by

GYAN

Gyan Publishing House
5, Ansari Road
Daryaganj, New Delhi-110002
Phone: 011-47034999, 9811692060
E-mail: books@gyanbooks.com

Distribution Network
gyanbooks.com
India, USA, Canada, UK, Australia

ISBN: 978-93-6780-354-7 (HB)

First Published, 1890

2nd Impression 2024

Printed at: Gyan Press, Delhi.

A PRIMER OF SPOKEN ENGLISH

Author: HENRY SWEET

Clarendon Press Series

A

PRIMER OF SPOKEN ENGLISH

SWEET

A PRIMER

OF

SPOKEN ENGLISH

BY

HENRY SWEET, M.A.

BALLIOL COLLEGE, OXFORD; HON. PH.D. HEIDELBERG

Oxford

AT THE CLARENDON PRESS

1890

PREFACE.

The present work is intended to supply the want of an English edition of my *Elementarbuch des gesprochenen Englisch*, published by the Clarendon Press in 1886, which has been very successful abroad. The grammar in this primer is simply a translation of that in the *Elementarbuch* with a few additions. The texts here given are, on the other hand, entirely new.

The object of this book is to give a faithful picture—a phonetic photograph—of educated spoken English as distinguished from vulgar and provincial English on the one hand, and literary English on the other hand. At the same time I must disclaim any intention of setting up a standard of spoken English. All I can do is to record those facts which are accessible to me—to describe that variety of spoken English of which I have a personal knowledge, that is, the educated speech of London and the district round it—the original home of Standard English both in its spoken and literary form. That literary English is the London dialect pure and simple has now been proved beyond a doubt by the investigations of the German Morsbach in his essay *Ueber den ursprung der neuenglischen schriftsprache* published in 1888, I having expressed the same view in the same year in my *History of English Sounds*. After London

English had become the official and literary language of the whole kingdom, it was natural that the same dialect in its spoken form should become the general speech of the educated classes, and that as centralization increased, it should preponderate more and more over the local dialects. But the unity of spoken English is still imperfect: it is still liable to be influenced by the local dialects—in London itself by the Cockney dialect, in Edinburgh by the Lothian Scotch dialect, and so on.

The comparative purity and correctness of the different varieties of spoken English is popularly estimated by the degree of approximation to the written language. But these comparisons are generally carried out in a one-sided and partial spirit. When an Englishman hears the distinct *r* and *gh* in the Broad Scotch *farther*, *night*, etc., he is apt to assume at once that Scotch English is more archaic than Southern English; but if he looks at the evidence on the other side, such forms as *ah ai oo*=*all one wool* will make him more inclined to believe what is the truth, namely that standard spoken English is, on the whole, quite as archaic, quite as correct and pure as any of its dialects—a truth which before the rise of modern philological dilettanteism and dialect-sentimentality no one ever thought of disputing.

Still more caution is required in attempting to estimate the comparative beauty and ugliness of the different varieties of spoken English. Our impressions on this point are so entirely the result of association that it is hardly possible to argue about them. The Cockney dialect seems very ugly to an educated English man or woman because he—and still more she—lives in perpetual terror of being taken for a Cockney, and a perpetual struggle to preserve that *h* which has now been lost in most of the local dialects of England, both North and South. Northern speakers often reproach Londoners with 'mincing affectation.' But the London pronunciation of the present day, so far from being mincing, is characterized by openness and broadness, which are carried to an extreme in the Cockney pronunciation of such words as *father*, *ask*, *no*. A century ago, when this reproach was first levelled against the Cockneys, there was really some foundation for it, for at that time the broad *a* in *father*, *ask* was represented by the thinner vowel in *man* lengthened, the Northern *ask* and *man* being at that time pronounced with the short sound of the *a* in *father*. When the sugar-merchants of Liverpool began to 'speak fine,' they eagerly adopted the thin Cockney *a* in *ask*, which many of their descendants keep, I believe, to the present day—long after this 'mincing' pronunciation has been discarded in the London dialect.

Another difficulty about setting up a standard of spoken English is that it changes from generation to generation, and is not absolutely uniform even among speakers of the same generation, living in the same place, and having the same social standing. Here, again, all I can do is to describe that form of the London dialect with which I am sufficiently familiar to enable me to deal with it satisfactorily. The only real familiarity we can have is with the language we speak ourselves. As soon as we go beyond that, and attempt to determine how other people speak—whether by observation or questioning—we make ourselves liable to fall into the grossest blunders. Of course, every self-observer has his personal equation, which he is bound to eliminate cautiously; and this I have done to the best of my power. Being partly of Scotch parentage—though I have lived most of my life near London—I have a few Scotticisms, such as *although* with sharp *th*, which sometimes crop up in rapid speech. Again, my pronunciation—like everyone else's—is in some cases more archaic, in others more advanced—more slovenly, more vulgar—than that of the majority of my contemporaries. When I pronounce *diphthong* with *p* instead of *f*, I have an impression that I am in the minority; and when I pronounce *either* and *neither* with the diphthong in *eye*, I have an impression that I am in the majority against those who pronounce these words with *ee*. But I have no means of proof that such is the case; and I know that if there were only one speaker in the world who said *eether*, he would probably assert confidently that this was the only pronunciation of the word—or at any rate the only 'correct' one. The fact is that the statements of ordinary educated people about their own pronunciation are generally not only valueless, but misleading. Thus I know as a fact that most educated speakers of Southern English insert an *r* in *idea(r) of*, *India(r) office* etc. in rapid speech, and I know that this habit, so far from dying out, is spreading to the Midlands; and yet they all obstinately deny it. The associations of the written language, and inability to deal with a phonetic notation, make most people incapable of recognizing a phonetic representation of their own pronunciation. When I showed my Elementarbuch to some English people, all of Northern extraction, they would not believe it represented my own pronunciation; they said it represented broad Cockney, of which they said there was not a trace in my own pronunciation.

I repeat then that this book is nothing but a contribution to our knowledge of spoken English—a knowledge which is still in its infancy, and can be advanced only by a number of other trained observers giving similar descriptions of their own pronunciation. It is only on the basis of such individual investigations that we can hope to settle what are the actual facts of spoken English in Great Britain, America, and Australasia. Till we know how we actually do speak, we cannot deal with the question how we ought to speak, and whether it is possible to reform our pronunciation, and take steps to preserve the unity of English speech all over the world.

Anyhow, I hope we shall have no more nonsense about my plain statement of facts being a blow aimed at correctness of speech. If my critics would only realize that this book, together with the Elementarbuch, is the only one in any language that gives adequate phonetic texts with the sentence-stress and intonation marked throughout, they would see that it is more profitable for them to discuss the plan and tendencies of the book itself than to abuse me for not suppressing and distorting facts which happen to shock their prejudices.

As regards the uses of this book, it is in the first place a contribution to English dialectology. It is further a contribution to the practical study of English both for natives and foreigners. English people will find a phonetic study of their own language the best possible preparation for the mastery of foreign languages, as well as for the study of general grammar and the science of language, including metre, the theory of verse and elocution, and literature generally. The very simple texts which come first will also be found suitable for teaching children to read phonetically.

The phonetic notation I have used is nearly the same as in the Elementarbuch, with some improvements, such as the substitution of *ŏ* for *ö*, as being easier to write. I have extended it to *ĭ*, which is as easy to write as the ordinary dotted *i*. I have also made the experiment of substituting word- for the stress-division of the Elementarbuch. I am still unable to decide which method is preferable.

In the grammar I have treated phonetics as briefly as possible, referring the reader to my *Primer of Phonetics*. I have as a general rule passed over briefly those points which are adequately treated in the conventional grammars, giving greater prominence to such totally new subjects as gradation, sentence-stress, etc.

To avoid monotony I have not written all the texts myself, but have also given pieces from older writers, modernizing and simplifying them where necessary.

HENRY SWEET.

NUNTON, 10 *January*, 1890.

CONTENTS.

GRAMMAR.

SOUNDS.

THE foundation of speech-sounds is breath from the lungs. In the formation of *voice* sounds, such as *aa* in 'father,' *v*, *g*, the vocal chords in the throat are brought together so as to vibrate. In *breath* or voiceless sounds, such as *h*, *f*, *k*, they are kept wide apart, so that the breath can pass through without hindrance. In *whispered* sounds they are brought closer together, but without vibration, so that the breath produces a rustling sound.

In *nasal* sounds, such as *m*, the passage into the nose is left open; in all other (non-nasal) sounds it is closed by pressing back the uvula or soft palate.

Quantity.

It is enough to distinguish three degrees of quantity: *short*, *half-long* and *long*. Half-long and long vowels are marked by doubling, except ε and ɔ, which never occur short. Long vowels occur only finally, as in *səə* 'sir,' and before voice consonants, as in *haad* 'hard'; before breath consonants they become half-long, as in *haat* 'heart'. Long vowels only occur in strong syllables (see Stress), in weak (and often in medium) syllables they become half-long or even short. Compare *səə!* with *-səə dgon* 'sir John', *jes -səə, jesə* 'yes sir',

The quantity of the diphthongs—all of which have the stress on the first element—follows the same laws; but in them the quantity is distributed about equally over both elements. Thus *rouz* 'rose' is pronounced almost *roo-uuz*, with both elements half-long, while in *roust* 'roast', the *o* and *u* together constitute a half-length.

Every final consonant is lengthened after a short strong vowel, remaining short after a long vowel or diphthong: compare *hit*=*hitt* with *haat*. If the final consonant is voiced, the length is distributed over vowel and consonant: *bæd* 'bad'=*bææddd* with both elements half-long. Short strong syllables occur only in such words as *betə* 'better', *silĭ* 'silly', where there is a single consonant followed by a weak vowel. So also in groups of words such as *pik ĭt ap* 'pick it up' where there is no pause between the weak vowel and the preceding consonant. If such a word or group is drawled, the length is thrown on to the weak vowel, as in *:whot ə pitiĭ* 'what a pity!' *stediĭ* 'steady!' All consonants are lengthened before another voice consonant, as in *bild* 'build', *penz* 'pens'=*billd, pennz*, compared with *bilt* 'built', *pens* 'pence'.

Double consonants are only written when the consonant is really pronounced double, as in *pennaif* 'pen-knife'.

Stress.

We distinguish four degrees of stress or force: *weak* (-), *medium* (:), *strong* (·), *emphatic* (;). The stress-marks are put before the element on which the stress begins, as in *:kontrə·dikt* 'contradict'.

Strong stress is not marked in monosyllabic words nor when it falls on the first syllable of longer words with the other syllables weak, as in *verĭ wel* 'very well'. The weak stress of 'light' vowels, such as *ə*, *ĭ*, is never marked, because these vowels only occur in weak syllables. Hence a 'heavy' vowel in a word otherwise made up of light vowels is assumed to have strong stress, unless otherwise marked: *rĭmembə* 'remember' = *rĭ·membə*, but *-ðei haid ðəm-selvz* 'they hide themselves.' If a word has two strong stresses (or a strong and an emphatic), both must be marked, as in *·an·duw* 'undo'. Such a word as *·plam·pudĭŋ* 'plum-pudding' is better written *plam pudĭŋ*.

If only one strong (or emphatic) stress is marked or implied in a polysyllabic word, any other heavy vowel symbols in the word are assumed to have weak or medium stress, between which it is often difficult to distinguish: *evrĭwheə* 'everywhere' = *·evrĭ-wheə*, *kontrə·dikt* = *:kontrə·dikt*; so also in *:whot ə kontrə;dikʃən* 'what a contradiction!'

If a strong stress mark is already implied, the addition of (·) is enough to mark emphatic stress instead of (;), as in *:whot ə ·pitĭ, rĭ·membə!*

The stress in every syllable diminishes progressively, so that in such a word as *kæt* 'cat' the *t* is uttered with less force than the *k*. After a long vowel, as in *kaat* 'cart' the diminution of stress is still more marked.

Intonation.

The tones are *level* (¯); *rising* (ˊ), as in *ˊwhot* 'what?'; *falling* (ˋ), as in *ˋnou* 'no!'; *falling-rising* (ˇ) or compound rise, as in *teik ˇkeə* 'take care!'; *rising-falling* or compound fall, as in *^ou* 'Oh!' as an expression of sarcasm. The tone-marks are put before the word they modify; if they modify a whole sentence, they are put at the end of it. The greater the interval of these tones, the more emphatic their meaning. Thus *ˊou* with a slight rise expresses slight curiosity or interest, with a more extensive rise astonishment.

If no tone-mark is written, a comma or ? implies a rising tone, a colon or semicolon a falling tone.

Organic Basis.

The general character of English speech depends on the following peculiarities of its organic basis:—

The tongue is broadened and flattened, and drawn back from the teeth (which it scarcely ever touches), and the fore part of it is hollowed out, which gives a dull sound, especially noticeable in *l*.

Rounded (labial) sounds, such as *w*, *uw* in 'who', are formed without any pouting of the lips.

In unrounded vowels, such as *aa*, *i*, the lips have a passive, neutral position. In the formation of front vowels such as *i*, *e*, there is no 'chinking' or spreading out of the corners of the mouth, by which in other languages their sound is made clearer.

Vowels.

In the vowels we distinguish three horizontal positions, or degrees of retraction of the tongue: *back*, *mixed*, *front*, and three vertical positions, or degrees of height (raising and lowering of the tongue): *high*, *mid*, *low*. Each of the vowels formed by the different combinations of retraction and height is either *narrow* or *wide*, according as the tongue and uvula are tense and convex, or relaxed and flattened. Lastly, all these vowels can be *rounded* by constriction of the mouth-opening, high vowels, such as *u* in *full*, having the narrowest, low vowels, such as *ɔ* in *fall*, the widest lip-opening, mid vowels such as *o*(*u*) in *no* an intermediate degree of closure. This gives 36 primary vowels, of which only some occur in English, as shown in the following table:—

-narrow			-wide		
1 high-back	4 high-mixed	7 high-front	10 high-back	13 high mixed	16 high-front i, ĭ : *city*
2 mid-back a : come	5 mid-mixed	8 mid front	11 mid-back aa : father	14 mid-mixed *ai*, ə : *i*sl*a*nd	17 mid-front e, *e*i : men, say
3 low-back	6 low-mixed əə : bird	9 low-front ɛ : care	12 low-back	15 low-mixed *a*u : how	18 low-front æ : man
-narrow-round			**-wide-round**		
19 high-back	22 high-mixed	25 high-front	28 high-back u, uw : put, who	31 high-mixed ŭ : value	34 high-front
20 mid-back	23 mid-mixed	26 mid-front	29 mid-back *o*u, *o*i : no, boy	32 mid-mixed ŏ : foll*o*w	35 mid-front
21 low-back ɔ : saw	24 low-mixed	27 low-front	30 low-back o : not	33 low-mixed	36 low-front

In perfectly weak syllables all vowels are modified in the direction of the mid-mixed-wide or mid-mixed-wide-round position, according as the vowel is non-rounded or rounded. In *ĭ* there is more lowering than retraction, so that this vowel is intermediate between *i* and *e*. In very rapid speech the retraction becomes more marked, so that it is sometimes difficult to distinguish *ĭ* from *ə*, as in 'possible' *posĭbl* or *posəbl*, which latter seems to be most usual. In rapid speech *ŏ* is partially or completely unrounded, so that it becomes *ə*, thus 'in a day or two' is pronounced either *ĭn ə dei ŏ :tuw* or *ĭn ə dei ə -tŭw* according to the speed of utterance. *ə* itself is often further weakened by being uttered with whisper instead of voice, when it comes immediately before a strong syllable, especially when it stands between two stopped consonants, as in *səptembə* 'September' (first vowel). These vowels, which occur only in weak or unstressed syllables, are called 'light' vowels, as opposed to the 'heavy' vowels *i*, *u*, *o*, etc. The most important light vowels are *ə*, *ĭ*, *ŭ*, *ŏ*, and the diphthongs formed with them: *əi*, *əu*, *ŏu*. But all the heavy vowels have special light forms, thus the two *æ*s in 'abstract' have not exactly the same sound, the light vowel in the second syllable being an approximation to *ə*. Such light vowels, for which no special sign is provided, may be marked by (-), when necessary, as in *æb-stræ-kt*=*æbstrăkt*.

The second elements of the diphthongs *ai*, *ei*, *oi*, *au*, are not full *i* and *u*, but rather *ĭ*, *ŏ*. In *ou* the second element combines the mid-tongue position of the *o* with the high lip-rounding of *u*, so that the tongue does not move during the formation of the diphthong. *ŏu* is formed analogously without any movement of the tongue, though here the extra rounding represented by the *u* is often slight and doubtful, the whole diphthong being much shortened. *ij* and *uw* are 'consonantal' diphthongs, although in *ij* the *j* is generally not full *j* in *you* but nearly *i*, the first element being lowered nearly to *ĭ*. In *iə* and *uə*, as in *fear*, *poor*, the first elements are slightly lowered. The first element of *ai* is more retracted than *ə*. *aa* and *ɔ* are not pure monophthongs; they might be written *aə*, *ɔŏ* (with length distributed over both elements, as in *ei*, *iə*, etc.). Hence it is often difficult to distinguish between *lɔ* 'law'=*lɔŏ* and *lɔə* 'lore'. Before a consonant both sounds are levelled under *ɔ*, as in *lɔd* 'laud', 'lord'.

The separate vowels are as follows, all those in weak syllables being examples of light vowels:

a (2) *as in* kam 'come', hambag 'humbug'.
aa (11) „ „ faaðə 'father', 'farther'.
ai (14) „ „ hai 'high'.
au (15) „ „ hau 'how'.
æ (18) „ „ æbstrækt 'abstract'.
e (17) „ „ men 'men', insekt 'insect'.
ei (17) „ „ sei 'say'.
ɛə (9) „ „ kɛə 'care'.
ə (14) „ „ təgeðə 'together'.
əi (14) „ „ twailəit 'twilight'.
əu (14) „ „ kompəund 'compound'.
əə (6) „ „ məəmə 'murmur'.
i (16) „ „ bit 'bit'.
ij (16) „ „ sij 'see', 'sea', ĭjsþetĭk 'æsthetic'.
iə (16) „ „ hiə 'here', 'hear'.
ĭ (16) „ „ sitĭ 'city'.
o (30) „ „ not 'not'.
ŏ (32) „ „ ŏktoubə 'October'.
oi (29) „ „ boi 'boy'.
ou (29) „ „ nou 'no', 'know'.

ŏu (32) *as in* folŏu 'follow'.
ɔ (21) „ „ fɔl 'fall'.
u (28) „ „ ful 'full'.
ŭ (31) „ „ væljŭ 'value'.
uw (28) „ „ fuwl 'fool', dʒŭwlai 'July'.
uə (28) „ „ puə 'poor'.

Consonants.

When it is necessary to show that a consonant is syllabic (has the function of a vowel), this is done by adding (-) or whatever stress-mark is required, as in *ijzl-ĭ* 'easily'. In *mjlk*—also pronounced *mjulk*—'milk' the *l* is syllabic.

By their articulation consonants are classed as (1) *open*, such as *r*, *s*; (2) *side*, such as *l*; (3) *stop*, such as *k*, *d*; (4) *nasal*, such as *m*. By position they are classed as (1) *back*, such as *k*, *ŋ* in 'sing'; (2) *front*, such as *j* in 'you'; (3) *point*, such as *t*, *þ*; (4) *lip*, such as *p*, *m*; (5) *lip-back*, such as *w*; (6) *lip-teeth*, such as *f*. The point consonants are subdivided into *gum*, such as *t*, *l* and *r*—which is formed further back than the others—and *teeth*, such as *þ* in 'thin'. The *blade*-consonant *s* is formed with the 'blade' or flattened point of the tongue; if the tongue is retracted from this position, and the point raised, we get the *blade-point* consonant *ʃ* in 'fish'.

The aspirate *h* only occurs before vowels and *j*, as in *huw* 'who', *hjuwdʒ* 'huge'.

All consonants can be breathed, voiced, and whispered, though some consonants do not occur breathed in English. Buzzes (voiced hisses) when final begin with voice and end in whisper, as in *sijz* 'sees'; if a stop or buzz precedes, the final consonant is entirely whispered, as in *fijldz* 'fields', *auə selvz* 'ourselves'. Final *g*, *d*, *b* are whispered after buzzes, as in *reizd* 'raised'; so also in *reidgd* 'raged', where the *g* is whispered as well as the final *d*.

The voiceless stops *k*, *t*, *p* are always followed by a 'breath-glide' or slight puff of breath, which is, of course, strongest at the beginning of a strong syllable. If followed by a voiced consonant, they devocalize its first half, as in *trai* 'try', *plijz* 'please' = *trhrai*, *plhlijz*. After non-initial stops, as in *bœtl* 'battle' there is less devocalization, and still less when the two consonants belong to different syllables, as *autlet* 'outlet'.

Initial voice stops, such as *g* in *gou* 'go', have hardly any vocality in the stop itself, voice being heard mainly in the 'glide' or transition to the vowel.

The only consonants whose notation requires special notice are the following:

dʒ	*as in*	dʒadʒ 'judge'.
ð	„ „	ðen 'then'.
j	„ „	jes 'yes'.
ŋ	„ „	siŋ 'sing'.
ʃ	„ „	fiʃ 'fish'.
tʃ	„ „	tʃəətʃ 'church'.
þ	„ „	þin 'thin'.
wh	„ „	whot 'what'.
ʒ	„ „	pleʒə 'pleasure'.

wh is generally pronounced *w*.

The following is a table of the English consonants:

	Throat	Back	Front	Gum	Teeth	Blade	Blade-Point	Lip	Back-Lip	Lip-Teeth
	Breathed									
Open	h				þ	s	ʃ		wh	f
Side										
Stop		k		t				p		
Nasal										
	Voiced									
Open			j		ð	z	ʒ		w	v
Side										
Stop		g		d				b		
Nasal		ŋ		n				m		

Sound-junction.

r only occurs before a vowel following it without any pause, as in *hiər ĭj iz* 'here he is'; elsewhere—that is before a consonant or a pause—it disappears leaving only the preceding *ə*, as *hĭj z hiə* 'he is here'. The *ə* is completely absorbed by a preceding *əə*, as in *əə, əərĭŋ* 'err', 'erring', and almost completely so by a preceding *aa*, as in *faa, faar əwei* 'far', 'far away' (p. 7). After *ɔ* the *ə* is kept finally, but dropt before the *r*, as in *pɔə, pɔə daun* 'pour', 'pour down', *pɔrĭŋ, pɔr aut* 'pouring', 'pour out', being also dropt before a consonant in the same word (p. 7), as in *pɔd* 'poured'. Short vowel + *r* occurs only medially, as in *spirĭt* 'spirit'.

The following are the combinations :—

ar : *harĭ* 'hurry'.
aa(r) : *staa* 'star', *staarĭ* 'starry'.
aiə(r) : *faiə* 'fire', *faiərĭ* 'fiery'.
auə(r) : *flauə* 'flower', 'flour', *flauərĭ* 'flowery'.
əə(r) : *əə* 'err', *əərĭŋ* 'erring'.
ir : *spirĭt* 'spirit'.
iə(r) : *hiə* 'here', 'hear', *hiərĭŋ* 'hearing'.
er : *verĭ* 'very'.
eiə(r) : *peiə* 'payer'.
ɛə(r) : *ɛə* 'air', *vɛərĭ* 'vary'.
ær : *nærŏu* 'narrow'.
uə(r) : *puə* 'poor', *kjuərĭəs* 'curious'.
ouə(r) : *louə* 'lower'.
ɔə, ɔr : *pɔə* 'pour', *pɔrĭŋ* 'pouring'.
or : *sorĭ* 'sorry'.
oiə(r) : *ĭndgoiə* 'enjoyer'.

eiə is often made into *ɛə*, as in *briklɛə* 'bricklayer', and *ouə* into *ɔə*, as in *lɔə* 'lower'.

r is frequent after *ə*, as in *aaftə, aaftər ɔl* 'after (all)', *sentʃəri* 'century'. In careless speech it is often added after *ə* before a vowel in words which are not written with *r*, as in *əidiər ŏv* 'idea of', *indjər ɔfĭs* 'India Office'.

The *n* of *ən* 'an' is dropt in the same way before a consonant: *ən enĭmĭ* 'an enemy', *ə mæn* 'a man'.

The vowels of *ðĭ* 'the' and *tŭ* 'to' are weakened to *ə* before a consonant: *ðĭ enĭmĭ, ðə mæn*; *tŭ ijt* 'to eat', *tə bed* 'to bed'.

When three consonants come together in different words, the middle one is often dropt, as in *ðə laas taim* 'the last time', *əi doun nou* 'I don't know'. *td* is often shortened to *d* in *si daun* 'sit down', etc.

There is sometimes partial assimilation—often together with consonant-dropping—as in *əi kaaŋ gou* 'I can't go', *-wĭj ʃl miʃʃŭ* 'we shall miss you'.

FORMS (ACCIDENCE).

Gradation.

Words that occur very frequently with weak stress often develope a *weak* form by the side of the original *strong* one. Thus we have the pairs of strong and weak forms *ʃæl* and *ʃəl*, *ðɛə(r)* and *ðər*, *iz* and *z*, *s*, as in *:whot ·ʃæl əi duẁ*, *whot ʃəl əi duẁ* 'what shall I do', *ðəz noubədĭ ðɛə* 'there is nobody there'; *:whot iz ĭt ĭj z tɔkĭŋ ə:baut̀* 'what is it he is talking about?'

The weak stage is mainly characterized by the light vowels *ə*, *ĭ*, *ŭ*, *ŏ*.

ə represents a variety of heavy vowels:

a: *əs* = *as* 'us'.

aa: *ə(r)* = *aa(r)* 'are'.

əə: *wə(r)* = *wəə(r)* 'were'.

e: *ðəm* = *ðem* 'them'.

ɛə: *ðə(r)* = *ðɛə(r)* 'there'.

æ: *ðət* = *ðæt* 'that'.

u: *ʃəd* = *ʃud* 'should'.

o: *wəz* = *woz* 'was'.

It also represents a further weakening of other light vowels in rapid or very familiar speech, as in *jə*, *jə(r)*=*jŭ*, *jŏ*, the strong forms of which are *juw*, *juə* 'you', 'your'.

ĭ represents *i*, as in *ĭt*=*it* 'it'. It is sometimes a further weakening of *ĭj*, as in *mĭ*=*mĭj*, strong *mij* 'me', but *ĭj* seems to be the usual weak form of *ij*.

ŭ—sometimes *ŭw*—represents *uw*, as in *jŭ*=*juw* 'you'.

ŏ represents *o* and *ɔ*, as in *ŏn*=*on* 'on', *ŏ(r)*=*ɔə*, *ɔr* 'or'.

əi, *əu*, *ŏu* represent *ai*, *au*, *ou* respectively.

Further stages of weakening are the dropping of vowels, as in *z*=*iz*, and of consonants, such as *h* in *ĭz*=*hiz* 'his', and *n* in *ən*=*ænd* 'and.' *h* in weak forms is kept only at the beginning of a sentence: *hĭj sɔ ĭm* 'he saw him'.

The strong *juə(r) juəz* 'your', 'yours' generally make their *u* into *ŏ*, giving *jŏə(r)*, *jŏəz*. This seems to be partly due to the lowering influence of the *ə*, partly to the analogy of the weak *jŏr*. They are the only words which have light vowels in strong-stressed syllables. *jɔə*, *jɔr*, *jɔz* may also be heard, and for convenience these are written for the strong forms.

Strong forms, on the contrary, often occur unstressed, such as *ðæt* (pronoun) in *əi nou -ðæt*, where it has the same weak stress as the weak *ðət* in *əi nou ðət ĭt s truw* 'I know that it is true'.

The following is a list of the most important weak forms ranged under the corresponding strong forms. It has not been thought necessary to include all the self-evident weakenings of *i* to *ĭ*, *ou* to *ŏu*, etc. Forms marked * occur only occasionally, or in special combinations.

aar 'are': *ə(r)*.

as 'us': *əs*; *s* in *lets* 'let us'.

æm 'am': *əm*; *m*.

***æn** 'an': *ən*.

***ænd** 'and': *ən* before consonants; *ənd* before vowels; often further shortened to *n*, as in *:bred n batə* 'bread and butter', and *m* after lip-consonants, as in *:kap m sɔsə* 'cup and saucer'.

æt 'at': *ət.*

***æz** 'as': *əz.*

bai 'by': *bəi*; **bə.*

bij 'be': *bĭj; bĭ.*

bijn 'been': *bĭjn; bĭn.*

daz 'does': *dəz.*

duw 'do': **də*, **d.*

***ðæn** 'than': *ðən.*

ðei aar 'they are': *ðɛə(r).*

ðem 'them': *ðəm*; *əm.*

ðɛə(r) 'their', 'there': *ðə(r).*

ðɛə(r) iz 'there is': *ðəz.*

***ðij** 'the': *ðĭ* before vowels; *ðə* before consonants.

***ei** 'a': *ə.*

fɔə, fɔr 'for': *fŏ(r)*; *fə(r).*

from 'from': *frəm.*

hæd 'had': *həd; əd; d.*

hæv 'have': *həv; əv; v.*

hæz 'has': *həz; əz; z, s*, the use of *əz, z, s*, follows the same rules as inflectional *s* (p. 16).

həə(r) 'her': *hə(r).*

hij 'he': *hĭj; ĭj.*

him 'him': *hĭm; ĭm.*

hiz 'his': *hĭz; ĭz.*

iz 'is': *ĭz; z, s*, the use of *ĭz, z, s* follows the rules of inflectional *s* (p. 16).

jŏə, jŏr 'your': *jŏ(r); jə(r).*

juw 'you': *jŭw; jŭ; jə.*

kæn 'can': *kən; kn.*

kud 'could': *kəd.*

mast 'must': *məst; məs.*

mij 'me': *mĭj; mĭ.*

***noə, nɔr** 'nor': *nŏ(r); nə(r).*

not 'not': *nt* only in verbal forms.

on 'on': *ŏn.*

ov 'of': *ŏv; əv; ə.*

***ɔə, ɔr** 'or': *ŏ(r); ə(r).*

sam 'some': *səm.*

satʃ 'such': *sətʃ.*

seint 'Saint', St.': *snt* before vowels, *sn* before consonants.

ʃud 'should': *ʃəd.*

ʃij 'she': *ʃĭj; ʃĭ.*

til 'till': *tĭl; tl.*

***tuw** 'to': *tŭ* before vowels, *tə* before consonants.

weə(r) 'were': *wə(r).*

wij 'we': *wĭj; wĭ.*

wil 'will': *əl, l.*

woz 'was': *wəz.*

wud 'would': *wəd; əd; d.*

Inflection of Nouns.

Besides the uninflected 'common form' (*hɔs* 'horse'), nouns have only one case—the genitive. The genitive singular ends in

(1) **-ĭz** after hisses and buzzes (*s, z; ʃ, ʒ*): *hɔsĭz* 'horse's'. *dʒɔdʒĭz* 'George's'.

(2) **-z** after the other voice sounds: *deiz* 'day's', *dʒonz* 'John's.'

(3) **-s** after the other breath consonants: *əəþs* 'earth's', *kæts* 'cat's'.

The regular plural is formed in the same way: *hɔsĭz* 'horses', *deiz* 'days', *kæts* 'cats'. Some words ending in *þ* and *ʃ* take *z* in the plur., and voice the *þ* and *ʃ*: *baaþ* 'bath', *baaðz*; *laif* 'life', *laivz*; *waif* 'wife', *waivz*. *haus* 'house' has plur. *hauzĭz*.

peni 'penny' has a regular plur. *penĭz*, and a collective plur. *pens* 'pence', in composition *-pəns*, as in *paundz, ʃilĭŋz ən pens, sikspəns*. New (regular) plurals are formed from these last: *tuw sikspənsĭz*. *iŋglĭʃmən* 'Englishman' has the plur. *ðĭ iŋglĭʃ* 'the English'; without *ðĭ* the plur. is the same as the sing.: *tuw iŋglĭʃmən* 'two Englishmen'. So also with ordinary names of nations ending in a hiss or buzz, such as *frenʃmən, welʃmən*; *tʃainəmən* 'Chinaman' has plur. *ðə ·tʃai·nijz* 'the Chinese'.

The following are wholly irregular:

(1) *oks, oksn* 'ox', 'oxen'.

(2) *tʃaild, tʃuldrən* 'child', 'children'.

(3) *ʃijp* 'sheep' and *-mən* '-men', as in *dgentlmən*, are unchanged in the plur.

(4) *fut, fijt* 'foot', 'feet'; *guws, gijs* 'goose', 'geese'; *mæn, men* 'man', 'men'; *maus, mais* 'mouse', 'mice'; *tuwþ, tijþ* 'tooth' 'teeth'; *wumən, wimĭn* 'woman', 'women'.

The regular gen. plur. is the same as the gen. sing.; in such words as *baaþ, haus* the gen. plur. is the same as the common form of the plur.; the irregular plurals add *ĭz, z*, or *s* to the plur. form: *gijsĭz, menz, ʃijps*.

Sing.	*Common.*	hɔs	laif	mæn
	Gen.	hɔsĭz	laifs	mænz
Plur.	*Common.*	hɔsĭz	laivz	men
	Gen.	hɔsĭz	laivz	menz.

Word-groups are often inflected like single words: *ðə tuw :mis smiþs, :kwijn vĭktɔriəz pælĭs; ðə mæn əi :sɔ jestədĭz faaðə.*

Comparison of Adjectives.

The comparative is formed by adding *-ə(r)*, the superlative by adding *-ĭst: big, bigə, bigĭst.* Many dissyllabic and nearly all longer adjectives are compared by prefixing *mɔə, mɔr*, and *moust: bjuwtĭfl, mɔə bjuwtĭfl, moust bjuwtĭfl.*

The following are irregular:

bæd 'bad' / il 'ill'	wəəs 'worse'	wəəst 'worst'
faa(r) 'far'	faaðə(r) 'farther' / fəəðə(r) 'further'	faaðĭst 'farthest' / fəəðĭst 'furthest'
ould 'old'	ouldə(r) 'older' / eldə(r) 'eldest'	ouldĭst 'oldest' / eldĭst 'eldest'
litl 'little'	les 'less'	lijst 'least'
gud 'good' / wel 'well'	betə 'better'	best 'best'
matʃ 'much' / menĭ 'many'	mɔə, mɔr 'more'	moust 'most'.

Numerals.

	Cardinal.	*Ordinal.*
1	wan 'one'	fəəst 'first'
2	tuw 'two'	sek(ə)nd 'second'
3	þrij 'three'	þəəd 'third'
4	fɔə, fɔr 'four'	fɔþ 'fourth'
5	faiv 'five'	fifþ 'fifth'
6	siks 'six'	siks(þ) 'sixth'
7	sevn 'seven'	sevnþ 'seventh'
8	eit 'eight'	eitþ 'eighth'
9	nain 'nine'	nainþ 'ninth'

10	ten 'ten'	tenþ 'tenth'
11	ĭlevn 'eleven'	ĭlevnþ 'eleventh'
12	twelv 'twelve'	twelfþ 'twelfth'
13	·þəə·tijn 'thirteen' ..	·þəə·tijnþ 'thirteenth'
14	·fɔ·tijn 'fourteen' ..	·fɔ·tijnþ
15	·fif·tijn 'fifteen'	·fif·tijnþ
16	·siks·tijn 'sixteen' ..	·siks·tijnþ
17	·sevn·tijn 'seventeen' ..	·sevn·tijnþ
18	·ei·tijn 'eighteen'	·ei·tijnþ
19	·nain·tijn 'nineteen' ..	·nain·tijnþ
20	twentĭ 'twenty'	twentĭĭþ 'twentieth'
21	twentĭ wan 'twenty-one'	twentĭ fəəst
22	twentĭ tuw 'twenty-two'	twentĭseknd
30	þəətĭ 'thirty'	þəətĭĭþ
40	fɔtĭ 'forty'	fɔtĭĭþ
50	fiftĭ 'fifty'	fiftĭĭþ
60	sikstĭ 'sixty'	sikstĭĭþ
70	sevntĭ 'seventy'	sevntĭĭþ
80	eitĭ 'eighty'	eitĭĭþ
90	naintĭ 'ninety'	naintĭĭþ
100	ə handrəd 'a hundred' ..	handrədþ 'hundredth'
101	ə handrəd n wan	handrəd n fəəst
200	tuw handrəd	tuw handrədþ
1,000	ə þauznd 'a thousand'	þauznþ 'thousandth'
2,000	tuw þauznd	tuw þauznþ
100,000	ə handrəd þauznd ..	handrəd þauznþ
1,000,000	ə miljən 'a million' ..	miljənþ 'millionth'.

In continuous counting the *-teen* numbers throw the stress on the first syllable—*þəətijn*, etc. (p. 29).

tuw and *þrij* shorten and modify their vowels when combined with *peni* and *pens*: *tapənĭ*, *tapəns*, *þripəns*.

Inflections of Pronouns.

(*a*) *Personal Pronouns.*

Sing. Nominative	ai 'I'		juw (jŭ) 'you'
Oblique	mij (mĭ) 'me'		juw (jŭ)
Plur. Nom.	wij (wĭ) 'we'		juw (jŭ)
Obl.	as (əs) 'us'		juw (jŭ)
Sing. Nom.	hij (ĭj) 'he'	it 'it'	ʃij (ʃĭ) 'she'
Obl.	him (ĭm) 'him'	it 'it'	həə(r) əər, əə 'her'
Plur. Nom.	ðei 'they'		
Obl.	ðem (ðəm, əm) 'them.'		

The forms in parentheses are the weak ones, which are more fully described under Gradation (p. 13).

The emphatic and reflexive form are:

Sing.	məiself 'myself'		jɔ·self 'yourself'
Plur.	əuəselvz 'ourselves'		jɔ·selvz 'yourselves'
Sing.	hĭmself 'himself'	ĭtself 'itself'	həə·self 'herself'
Plur.	ðəmselvz 'themselves'.		

To which must be added the indefinite *wənself* 'oneself', which is only reflexive.

When used emphatically these compounds take strong stress on the second element; when used reflexively both elements have weak stress, except when the reflexive pronoun is emphatic: *hĭj woʃt ĭt ĭmself; hĭj woʃt ĭm-self ɔl ouvə; hĭj woʃt ĭm;self.*

(*b*) *Interrogative Pronouns.*

	Masc. & Fem.	*Neut.*
Nom.	huw 'who'	whot 'what'
Obl.	huw, huwm 'whom'	whot.

(*c*) *Possessive Pronouns.*

Conjoint: *mai* 'my', *auə(r)* 'our'; *jɔə(r)* 'your'; *hiz* 'his', *its* 'its', *həə(r)* 'her', *ðɛər* (*ðər*) 'their'; *huwz* 'whose'.

Absolute: *main* 'mine', *auəz* 'ours'; *jɔəz* 'yours'; *hiz* 'his', *its* 'its', *həəz* 'hers', *ðɛəz* 'theirs'; *huwz* 'whose'.

(*d*) *Demonstrative Pronouns.*

Sing.	ðis 'this'	ðæt 'that'
Plur.	ðijz 'these'	ðouz 'those'.

(*e*) *Indefinite Pronouns.*

wan 'one', *aðə(r)* 'other' and their compounds, together with *enĭbodĭ* 'anybody', have a genitive or possessive in **-z**: *wanz*, *aðəz*, *enĭbodĭz*. *wanz*, *aðəz* are also plurals.

fjuw 'few' takes the indef. article: *ə fjuw buks*, *ə fjuw ə(v) ðə letəz*. So also with *menĭ* 'many' in *ə greit ·menĭ* (*buks*). *ɔl* 'all' takes the def. article between itself and its noun: *ɔl ðə taim*, *ɔl ðə men*.

Inflections of Verbs.

(A) *Consonantal Class.*

Indicative.

		Present.	*Preterite.*
Sing.	1	kɔl 'call'	kɔld 'called'
,,	2	kɔl	kɔld
,,	3	kɔlz 'calls'	kɔld
Plur.		kɔl	kɔld.

Imperative kɔl. *Infinitive* kɔl.

Present Participle (*Gerund*) kɔlĭŋ 'calling'.

Pret. Participle kɔld.

The subjunctive differs from the indicative only in having its 3 sing. uninflected—*kɔl.*

The unmodified form *kɔl* is called the 'common form'.

The addition of the inflectional *z* follows the same rules as with the nouns: *sijzĭz, fiʃĭz, kɔlz, stops* 'seizes,' 'fishes', 'calls', 'stops'. *sei* 'say' has vowel-change: *sez* 'says'.

The preterite ending appears as

(1) *-ĭd* after *t* and *d*: *dĭlaitĭd* 'delighted', *nodĭd* 'nodded'.

(2) *-d* after the other voice sounds: *pleid* 'played', *seivd* 'saved', *drægd* 'dragged'.

(3) *-t* after the other breath consonants: *puʃt* 'pushed', *lukt* 'looked'. After voice consonants in *bəənt* 'burned', *dwelt, ləənt, spoilt.*

The following change final *d* into *t*: *bend, bent; bild, bilt* 'build'; *lend, lent; send, sent; spend, spent.*

The following add *d* or *t* with vowel-change:

d: *hiə(r)* 'hear', *həəd.* *sei* 'say', *sed.* *sel, sould; tel, tould.*

t: *krijp* 'creep', *krept; drijm* 'dream', *dremt; fijl* 'feel', *felt; kijp* 'keep', *kept; lijv* 'leave', *left; mijn* 'mean', *ment; slijp* 'sleep', *slept; swijp* 'sweep', *swept.* *bai* 'buy', *bɔt; luwz* 'lose', *lɔst.*

The following drop their final consonant before the preterite-ending, with vowel-change before *t*:

d: *meik* 'make', *meid.*

t: *briŋ, brɔt* 'brought'; *þiŋk, þɔt.* *sijk* 'seek', *sɔt; tijtʃ* 'teach', *tɔt.* *kætʃ* 'catch', *kɔt.*

aask 'ask' only drops the *k*: *aast.*

(B) *Vocalic Class.*

This class differs from the former only in the formation of the pret. and pret. partic. It includes only a limited number of verbs.

(*a*) *Pret. part. in* -n.

(α) *Different vowels in pret. and pret. partic.*

giv 'give', *geiv, givn.*

draiv 'drive', *drouv, drivn; raid, roud, ridn; rait* 'write', *rout, ritn; raiz, rouz, rizn.*

flai 'fly', *fluw* 'flew', *floun* 'flown'.

ijt 'eat', *et* 'ate', *ijtn. sij* 'see', *sɔ* 'saw', *sijn*; *ʃeik* 'shake', *ʃuk* 'shook', *ʃeikn; teik, tuk, teikn.*

blou 'blow', *bluw* 'blew', *bloun; grou, gruw, groun; nou* 'know', *njuw, noun; þrou, þruw, þroun. drɔ* 'draw', *druw, drɔn.*

(β) *Same vowels in pret. and pret. partic.*

lai 'lie', *lei* 'lay', *lein* 'lain'. *haid, hid, hidn; bait, bit, bitn.*

frijz 'freeze', *frouz, frouzn; spijk* 'speak', *spouk, spoukn; stijl* 'steal', *stoul, stouln; wijv* 'weave', *wouv, wouvn. breik* 'break', *brouk, broukn. tʃuwz* 'choose', *tʃouz, tʃouzn.*

tred 'tread', *trod, trodn.*

bɛə(r) 'bear', *bɔə, bɔr, bɔn; swɛə(r), swɔə, swɔr, swɔn; tɛə(r), tɔə, tɔr, tɔn; wɛə(r), wɔə, wɔr, wɔn.*

bijt 'beat', *bijt, bijtn.*

(*b*) *Pret. partic. without* -n.

(*a*) *Different vowels in pret. and pret. partic.*

bĭgin, bĭgæn, bĭgan ; driŋk, dræŋk, draŋk ; riŋ, ræŋ, raŋ ; siŋ, sæŋ, saŋ ; siŋk, sæŋk, saŋk ; spriŋ, spræŋ, spraŋ ; swim, swæm, swam.

kam 'come', *keim, kam.* *ran* 'run', *ræn, ran.*

(β) *Same vowels in pret. and pret. partic.*

dig, dag ; kliŋ, klaŋ ; spin, span ; stik 'stick', *stak ; swiŋ, swaŋ ; win, wan. hæŋ, haŋ. straik, strak.*

baind 'bind', *baund* 'bound'; *faind, faund; graind, graund ; waind, waund.*

lait 'light', *lit.*

hould 'hold', *held. blijd* 'bleed', *bled ; fijd* 'feed', *fed ; lijd* 'lead', *led ; mijt* 'meet', *met ; rijd* 'read', *red* 'read'.

sit, sæt ; spit, spæt.

weik 'wake' *wouk.* So also *əweik* 'awake'.

get, got. ʃain 'shine', *ʃon* 'shone'. *ʃuwt* 'shoot', *ʃot. ʃait* 'fight', *ʃɔt* 'fought'.

With consonant-dropping: *stænd* 'stand', *stud* 'stood'.

The following keep the same vowel in the common form, pret., and pret. partic.:

spred 'spread'.

bəəst 'burst'. *həət* 'hurt'. *hit. kaast* 'cast'. *kat* 'cut'. *kɔst* 'cost'. *put* 'put'. *ʃat* 'shut'. *set.*

Some have a *d*-pret., and a pret. partic. in -*n* :

ʃou 'show', *ʃoud, ʃoun. sou* 'sow', *soud, soun. swel, sweld, swouln. gou* 'go', *went, gɔn, gon* 'gone' is made up of two different verbs.

(C) *Defective Verbs.*

These verbs have only pres. and pret., and, as they take no inflectional *s*, they make no distinction between indicative and subjunctive; they have no infinitive or participle; *mast* and *ɔt* have no pret.

All these verbs—as also the Anomalous Verbs (see under D) —have negative forms in *-nt*, often with vowel-change and consonant dropping. Weak forms are in parentheses.

mei 'may', *meint; mait, maitnt.*

wil 'will' (*l; ail, juwl* &c.), *wount; wud* 'would' (*əd; aid, juwd, hijd, ʃijd, itəd, wijd, ðeid*), *wudnt.*

ʃæl 'shall' (*ʃəl; aiʃəl, juwʃəl* &c.) *ʃaant; ʃud* (*ʃəd*) *ʃudnt.*

mast 'must' (*məst, məs*), *masnt.*

kæn 'can' (*kən*), *kaant; kud* (*kəd*), *kudnt.*

ɔt 'ought', *ɔtnt.*

dɛə(r) 'dare' and *nijd* 'need' agree with these verbs in taking no *s* in the 3 sing. pres.; they hardly occur except in the negative forms of the pres.; *hĭj dɛənt, hĭj nijdnt. dɛə(r)* in the sense of 'challenge' is regular: *hĭj dɛəz ĭm tə duw ĭt.*

(D) *Anomalous Verbs.*

(1) **bij** 'be'.[1]

		Indicative.	*Subjunctive.*
Pres. Sing.	1	æm (m; aim); eint	bij
	2	aar (ər; jɔə, jɔr); eint	bij
	3	iz (z, s; hijz, ʃijz, its); iznt	bij.
Plur.		aar (ər; wiər, jɔr &c., ðɛər); eint	bij.

[1] Written forms: *am, are, is; was, were; being; been.*

		Indicative.	*Subjunctive.*
Pret. Sing.	1	woz (wəz), woznt	wəər (wər), wəənt
	2	wəər (wər), wəənt	wəər (wər), wəənt
	3	woz (wəz), woznt	wəər (wər), wəənt.
Plur.		wəər (wər), wəənt	wəər (wər), wəənt.
Imper.		bij.	*Infin.* bij.
Pres. Partic.		bijĭŋ.	*Pret. Partic.* bijn (bĭn).

(2) **hæv** 'have'.[1]

Pres. Sing.	1	hæv (əv, v; aiv), hævnt	
	2	hæv (əv, v; juwv), hævnt	
	3	hæz (əz, z, s; hijz, ʃijz, its), hæznt.	
Plur.		hæv (əv, v; wijv, juwv, ðeiv), hævnt.	
Pret. Sing.	1	hæd (əd, d; aid), hædnt	
	2	hæd (əd, d; juwd), hædnt	
	3	hæd (əd, d; hijd, ʃijd, itəd), hædnt.	
Plur.		hæd (əd, d; wijd, juwd, ðeid), hædnt.	
Imper.		hæv (həv).	*Infin.* hæv (həv).
Pres. Part.		hævĭŋ.	*Pret. Partic.* hæd (həd).

(3) **duw** 'do'.[2]

		Pres.	*Pret.*
Sing.	1	duw, dount	did, didnt
	2	duw, dount	did, didnt
	3	daz, daznt	did, didnt.
Plur.		duw, dount	did, didnt.
Imper.		duw.	*Infin.* duw.
Pres. Partic.		duwĭŋ.	*Pret. Partic.* dan.

---

1 Written forms: *has, had, having.*

2 Written forms: *does, did, doing, done.*

SYNTAX.

Stress.

(a) *Composition-stress.*

The general logical principle which governs stress in compounds is that even stress (·*a*·*a*) separates, uneven stress (generally ·*aa*, less frequently *a*·*a*) combines the ideas expressed in the compound.

Accordingly in the combination noun + noun even stress is employed when the first element has the function of a simple attributive and could be represented by an adjective, as in the following examples:

bou windŏu ; rok solt. stijl pen ; plam pudiŋ. gaadn wɔl. ijvnĭŋ staa. mæn kuk. hed weitə.

The most important exceptions are the names of natural objects, which take the stress ·*aa* in order to show that the two words together express a single idea: *gouldfiʃ ; batəflai ; æpltrij ; sænstoun.* Hence the distinction between *blæk bəəd* and *blækbəəd.* Note that compounds with *strijt* have the ·*aa* stress, as in *oksfədstrijt, haistrijt,* whilst names formed with *roud, skwɛə,* etc., have even stress: *oksfəd roud, paak lein, hænəvə skwɛə.*

If the composition expresses a causal relation of any kind, an action or a phenomenon, the ·*aa* stress is employed:

reinbou. təbækŏusmouk. stijmbout. flauəpot. mjuwzĭkmaastə. wəkĭŋĭkskəəʃən. bukbaində. əəþkweik.

In the combination adj. (adv.) + adj. even stress is usual: *gud lukĭŋ, haad boild, twentĭ faiv.*

Even stress occurs even in inseparable compounds, as in *·an·duw, ·mis·dʒadʒ, ·þəə·tijn*, etc., and in other words where the inseparable element has a strongly marked meaning. Even stress occurs even in simple words of more than one syllable, especially in interjections, such as *·hal·lou, ·braa·vou*, and in foreign names, such as *·bəə·lin, ·tʃai·nijz.*

When an even-stressed compound (or polysyllable) is used attributively before a noun, it takes the *·aa* stress: *ə gudneitʃəd felŏu* (but *hĭj z gud neitʃəd*); *haadboild egz; þəətijn men; bəəlĭn wul.* Compare also *ə sevn ə:klok dinə* with *wĭj dain əl sevn əklok.*

The stress *a·a* occurs especially in combinations of nouns with *ov* and *ænd:*

bilə(v)·fɛə, mænə(v)ðə·wəəld; kapm·səsə, naifn·fək.

So also in combinations of titles with names, as in *:mistə smiþ, :mis robətsn, :faamə hjuwz.* Also in exclamations, as in *·gud mənĭŋ*, or when a railway porter calls out *blæk·(h)ijþ* (but *blækhijþ steiʃən*).

(*b*) *Sentence-stress.*

Sentence-stress has a variety of functions; the most important types are the following:

(1) The **emphatic** stress. The general principle of sentence-stress is to stress the logically prominent words—those which are most indispensable for expressing the sense. In such a sentence as *əi :got wet* the first word is understood from the context, and the second is a mere connecting word,

so the stress necessarily falls on *wet* by what may be called *negative* emphasis; but in *luk həu ;wet əi -æm* there is increased stress on *wet* which gives it the meaning of 'very wet'; this is *positive* emphasis, or emphasis proper. All words that express new ideas are more or less emphatic; while words that express ideas already familiar or that can be taken for granted are unemphatic: *ə dʒəəmən :keim tə landən . . . ðə :dʒəəmən left :landən, ən :went tə livəpuwl.*

(2) The **intensive** stress, thrown on such words as *verĭ*, etc., even when they are not logically prominent: *əi ;kwait əgrij wĭð jŭ. jŭw l kætʃ jŏ ;deþ əv kould.*

(3) The **contrasting** stress: *ðə taunmaus ən ðə kantrĭmaus. þəətijn', fɔtijn', fiftijn\`* (in counting; but when isolated, *·þəətijn*, etc., as in the answer to the question *:hau ould ə jŭ\`*).

(4) The **modifying** stress: *ðĭ əəþ s raund; ĭt s not ;kwait :raund, bət ə :litl flætnd. hĭj z not ĭg:zæktlĭ ən iŋglĭʃmən; hĭj z ə ;welʃmən.*

(5) The **grouping** stress: *ʃəl wĭj smouk ə ;paip tə:geðə'. əi kaaŋ -get ;rid əv ĭm. əi nevə sɔ jŭ ĭn ə dres ;kout bĭ:fɔə.* Here *paiptəgeðə*, etc. are made into a kind of compound by throwing the stress on to the first element, just as in *gudneitʃəd felŏu*, etc.; compare the even stress in *ʃəl wĭj smouk ə paip\`; əi kaaŋ -get əwei; əi nevə sɔ jŭ ĭn ə dres kout.*

(6) The **distributed** stress. There are some formal connecting words, such as 'be' used as a copula, which have no meaning in themselves, and therefore are incapable of logical emphasis. Hence a strong stress thrown on such words is felt as equivalent to emphasizing the whole sentence, as in *:whot ;aa jŭ duwĭŋ\`* 'what are you doing!'

In the combination of adjectives (both attributive and predicative) with nouns, and of adverbs of marked meaning with other words, even stress is the rule: *ə big blæk dog; ĭt s haadlĭ taim tə gou -jet; ɔi m kwait redĭ; ĭt reinz haad.* This is especially the case in negative combinations: *ɔi þiŋk not* (compare *ɔi þiŋk sŏu*); *ɔi kaaŋ gou* (compare *ɔi kən duw ĭt təmorŏu*).

But if a noun acts as object to a verb with which it is intimately connected, so that a kind of compound is formed, the noun takes the stronger stress: *tə :ran ə reis; tə :spijk il əv :eniwan.*

If three strong-stressed words come together, the stress of the middle one is often reduced, especially if they are monosyllabic: compare *plam pudĭŋ* with *iŋglĭʃ :plam pudĭŋ; faiv minĭts* with *faiv :minĭts tə ten.*

This is especially the case in rapid speech, which is less favorable to even stress than slow speech. If two even-stressed syllables come together at the end of a sentence, the tendency is to throw the stress forward in rapid speech, so that such a word as *·tʃai·nijz* tends to *:tʃai·nijz.*

Logically subordinate words generally have weak stress, such as the articles, prepositions, auxiliary verbs, and many pronouns and particles. (For the accompanying sound-changes see p. 13).

Nouns and verbs—and sometimes adjectives—of subordinate meaning are treated in the same way, nouns such as *þiŋ*, *kaind*, *steit*, *paat*, verbs such as *hæv*, *get*, *meik*, *gou*: *ðə fəəst þĭŋ ɔi sɔ; :samþĭŋ ə(v) ðæt kəind; ĭn ðə :steit əv veipə; sam -paats əv iŋglənd; tə -hæv ðə plegə; tə :get bæk; tə -meik ə noiz.*

Many nouns and verbs lose their stress when enclitic: *:aa jŭ :gouĭŋ houm :dgon? jes (s)ə. səm bred plĭjz! :jɔə ðə doktər ɔi sə:pouz?\ ĭt s leit ĭznt ĭt?*

Under emphatic, contrasting, etc. stress almost any weak word can receive strong stress. Even the definite article may have strong stress in such a sentence as *ðæt s ;ðij :þing tə duw!* In this way *doublets* are often formed with special divergences of meaning and function:

hæv='must'; *-hæv*='cause', 'let'; *həv* auxiliary verb. *jŭw l hæv tə -hæv jŏ hɛə :kat.*

The weak forms of the auxiliaries occur only before the chief verb: compare *əi ʃəl gou* with *əi þiŋk əi -ʃæl;* and in the case of *bij* before the predicate: compare *hĭj z ə fuwl* with *:whot ə fuwl ĭj ĭz.* Isolated (absolute) auxiliaries often have strong stress, especially *iz* after demonstrative and interrogative words: *:huw iz ĭj?`; əi wandə :whɛər ĭj iz.* Also in answers and similar statements: *ĭz ĭj redi? əi ĭkspekt ĭj iz; wĭl ĭj duw ĭt? əi doun :nou -wheðər ĭj wil ŏ not.* Compare with the last: *əi doun :nou -wheðər ĭj l duw ĭt ŏ not.*

whot adjective, *:whot* (*whŏt*) noun: *whot taim ĭz ĭt?`; :whot s ðə taim?`.*

sam with strong stress is a quantitative word: *wĭð sam difĭkltĭ; sam :pĭjpl þiŋk sŏu.* In the partitive meaning of 'a little', French *de*, it is weakened to *səm: səm wɔtə; sə(m) mɔə bred!*

ĭnaf has weak stress when it follows its noun; otherwise it has strong stress: *gud ĭ-naf; bred ĭ-naf* but *inaf bred, inaf ə(v) ðis!*

ðɛər in its full meaning occurs both with strong and weak stress: *ðɛər ĭj iz!; əi sɔ ĭm -ðɛə jestədĭ.* The weak *ðər* occurs only in the combination *ðər iz*, etc., where it ceases to express locality: *ðə z naþĭŋ tə duw.*

when interrogative; *-when* relative: *əi ʃəl sij ĭm -when ĭj :kamz bæk, bət əi doun :nou when ĭj z kamĭŋ.*

Intonation.

Of the two simple tones, the rising (and the level) is interrogative or expectant (suspensive), the falling affirmative or conclusive.

Hence asserting and commanding sentences have the falling tone, as in *əi m redĭ*\ 'I am ready', *kam hiə*\ 'come here!'.

Direct questions, begun with a verb, have the rising tone: *ĭz ĭj redĭ*′ 'is he ready?'; *d jŭw nou ĭf ĭj z kamĭŋ*′ 'do you know if he is coming?'. But questions which are begun with an interrogative word have the falling tone, because they can be regarded as commands: *:whot s ðə mætə*\ 'what is the matter?'; *əi wandə :when ĭj z kamĭŋ*\ 'I wonder when he is coming'. So also disjunctive questions: *-aa jŭ kamĭŋ ŏ not*\ 'are you coming or not?'; *dəz ĭj liv ĭn landən*′ *ŏr ĭn ðə kantrĭ*\ 'does he live in London or in the country?'. If a sentence beginning with an interrogative word is repeated, it takes the rising tone, and the interrogative word takes the emphatic stress: compare *:huw iz ĭj*\ 'who is he?' with *;huw ĭz ĭj*′ ? *;huw dĭd jŭ sei ĭj woz*′.

Statements and commands are often uttered with rising tone, not only to characterize them as questionable and uncertain, but also in order to soften down a command, a refusal, a contradiction, an objection, etc.: *ĭz ĭt fain*′ 'is it fine?', *jes*′, *ĭt s pritĭ fain*′ 'yes, it is pretty fine' (compare *jes*\, *ĭt :luks :kwait setld*\ 'yes, it looks quite settled'); *səm mɔə tij*′ 'some more tea?', *nou þæŋk jŭ*′ 'no thank you'. *jŏ frend z leit*\ 'your friend is late'; *ĭt s not leit*′ : *ĭt s ounlĭ faiv*′ 'it is not late: it is only five'. The rising tone often serves only to give a character of cheerfulness or geniality to the conversation: *wel′, gud bai′; houp tə sij jŭ ə:gen suwn′* 'well, good-bye; hope to see you again soon'.

If, on the contrary, an interrogative sentence is uttered with a falling instead of its normal rising tone, it expresses command, impatience, etc.: *;wil jŭ duw əz jŏ tould* 'will you do as you are told!' *;aa jŭ redĭ* 'are you ready?' In such cases the auxiliary verb generally takes emphatic stress.

In the compound tones the second element determines the general meaning of the whole tone, and the first element only modifies it: the compound rise expresses doubt of some implied statement, expresses caution, warning, contrast, etc., while the compound fall hints at a doubt and disposes of it by a dogmatic assertion, and so expresses obstinacy, sarcasm, contempt, etc.

. *teik ᵛkɛə* 'take care!' *ᵛ;ai wount trai ĭt′; ᵛjuw -mei′* 'I will not try it; you may'. *ðə dinə wəz verĭ gud\, woz nt ĭt* 'the dinner was very good, was not it?' *ðə ᵛwain wəz bæd′* 'the wine was bad'.

ᵛai kən duw ĭt′ 'I can do it'. *^juw* 'you!' *əi sə:pouz əi :ɔt tŭ əpolədʒəiz* 'I suppose I ought to apologize'. *əi ʃəd ^þiŋk sŏu* 'I should think so!' *:ʃæl wĭ -hæv taim′* 'shall we have time?' *^ou -jes* 'oh yes!'

Nouns.

Gender.

Grammatical gender in English is almost exclusively marked by the pronouns referring to nouns, such as *hij*, *hiz* etc.

As a general rule nouns denoting male beings are *masculine*, those denoting female beings are *feminine*, all others being *neuter*.

As regards the gender of nouns denoting living beings it is to be noted that *tʃaild* 'child' is sometimes neuter. Names of animals are generally neuter, but often also masc. or fem. without regard to the sex of the individual animal. Thus *dog*, *hɔs* 'horse', *fiʃ* 'fish', *kənɛəri* 'canary' are generally masc., while *kæt* 'cat', *hɛə* 'hare', *pærət* 'parrot' are generally feminine. The greater the interest taken in the animal the more the personal genders are employed.

Names of things are often personified. *ʃip* 'ship', *bout* 'boat', *engin* 'engine' are fem., the names of smaller objects are often masc., such as *wotʃ* 'watch', *paip* 'pipe', but only in lively speech. It is to be observed that only artificial objects are personified; the names of natural objects which cannot be directly employed as tools etc., and of abstract ideas, are only referred to as *it*, such as *san* 'sun', *muwn* 'moon', *skai* 'sky', *sij* 'sea', *iŋglənd* 'England', *karĭdʒ* 'courage', *saiəns* 'science'.

Cases.

The common form corresponds to the nominative, accusative and dative cases in such languages as German: *ðæt mæn geiv məi braðər ən orĭnʒ* 'that man gave my brother an orange'.

The common form has a peculiar adjectival use: *jŭw wud nt :piŋk ðijz -tuw tʃuldrən wər ĭgzæktlĭ ðə seim eidʒ* 'you (=one) would not think these two children were exactly the same age'; *whot kalə ʃəl əi peint jŏ dɔə* 'what colour shall I paint your door?' *ĭt s nou :juws nokĭŋ* 'it is no use knocking (at the door)'.

The genitive is often used elliptically, especially after a

preposition, where the idea of 'house', etc. is to be supplied: *əi m stopĭŋ ət məi aŋklz* 'I am stopping at my uncle's'.

Number.

Many collective nouns, especially names of fishes and birds, are unchanged in the plural: *tə kætʃ fiʃ* 'to catch fish'.

So also some names of measures, etc. after numerals, especially when such a group is used attributively: *tuw dazn* 'two dozen'; *ə ten :paund nout* 'a ten pound note'.

Adjectives.

If an adjective or adjectival word or word-group stands alone without direct reference to a noun, it is followed by a weak *wan* 'one', which serves as a prop-word, and is inflected like a noun: *giv mĭj ə buk`—ən int(ə)restĭŋ -wan`* 'give me a book—an interesting one'; *tuw :dazn penĭ :stæmps, ənd ə dazn :tapəns heipnĭ -wanz* 'two dozen penny stamps and a dozen twopence halfpenny ones'.

The superlative is generally used instead of the comparative in comparing two objects: *hiər ə tuw rouds`; əi wandə :whitʃ ĭz ðə ʃətĭst`* 'here are two roads; I wonder which is the shortest'.

When such groups as *ðis :kaind əv*, *ðæt :sət əv* are joined to a noun in the plur., *ðis* and *ðæt* are also put in the plur.: *əi dount :laik ðijz :kaind əv æplz sŏu wel əz ðouz wĭj -hæd jestədĭ* 'I do not like these kind of apples so well as those we had yesterday'.

Pronouns.

The oblique case of the personal pronouns correspond to the accus. and dat. of such languages as German: *giv ĭt ĭm* 'give it him!'

The nom. *ai* is only used in immediate agreement with a verb; when used absolutely, *mij* is substituted for it by the formal analogy of *hij*, *wij*, *ʃij*, which are used absolutely as well as dependently: *ĭt s hij*, *ĭt s mij* 'it is he', 'it is me'; *huw z ðɛə*\ 'who is there?' *mij*.

The indefinite pronoun (French *on*) is generally expressed by *juw*: *ðə rait bæŋk əv ə rivə z ŏn jŏ rait said -when jŭ :stænd wĭð jŏ feis tŭ ĭts mauþ ən jŏ bæk tŭ ĭts sɔs* 'the right bank of a river is on your right side when you stand with your face to its mouth, and your back to its source'. Less frequently by *wan*: *ĭt rĭmaindz -wan əv :wan əv :mistə ;pikwĭks ədventʃəz* 'it reminds one of one of Mr. Pickwick's adventures'. Occasionally by *wij*: *:when beibĭz laaf, wĭj nou -ðɛə plijzd, ən :when -ðei krai, wĭj nou -ðɛər ĭn ə bæd tempə -ɔ ðət :sampĭŋ z roŋ wĭ ðəm* 'when babies laugh, we know they are pleased, and when they cry, we know they are in a bad temper, or that something is wrong with them'. *ðei* is used in *-ðei sei* 'they say'.

Singular indefinite pronouns, such as *eniwan*, *evrĭbodĭ*, *huw·evə*, are referred to with *ðei* to avoid the necessity of distinguishing between *hij* and *ʃij*: *ĭf eniwan kɔlz, tel ðəm əil bĭj bæk ĭn haaf ən auə* 'if anyone calls, tell them I will be back in half an hour'.

In some phrases the simple personal pronoun is used reflexively—*mai* instead of *məiself*: *əim :gouĭŋ tə :luk əbaut mĭ ə :litl* 'I am going to look about me a little'.

In such combinations as *əv main* the possessive pronoun is used instead of the obl. case of the personal pronoun: *hĭj z ə frend əv məin* 'he is a friend of mine'.

A relative pronoun in the function of an accusative is regularly dropped: *;jɔə ðə mæn əi wont* 'you are the man I want!'; *ðə z sampĭŋ əbaut ĭm əi dount laik* 'there is something about him I do not like'. A nominatival relative is also occasionally dropped: *huw z :ðæt dʒest ræŋ*\` 'who is that just rang?'

Verbs.

The conjugation of the verbs is effected partly by inflection, partly with auxiliaries. The following paradigm gives a general view of these forms and their relations to one another:

	ACTIVE.	PASSIVE.
	Indicative.	
Present	əi sij 'I see'	əim sijn
definite Pres.	əim sijĭŋ	əim bĭjĭŋ sijn
Preterite	əi sɔ	əi wəz sijn
def. Pret.	əi wəz sijĭŋ	əi wəz bĭjĭŋ sĭjn
Perfect	əiv sijn	əiv bĭjn sijn
def. Perf.	əiv bĭjn sijĭŋ	əiv bĭjn bĭjĭŋ sijn
Pluperfect	əid sijn	əid bĭjn sijn
def. Plup.	əid bĭjn sijĭŋ	əid bĭjn bĭjĭŋ sijn
Future	əi ʃl sij	əi ʃl bĭ sijn
def. Fut.	əi ʃl bĭ sijĭŋ	əi ʃl bĭ bĭjĭŋ sijn
Fut. Pret.	əi ʃəd sij	əi ʃəd bĭ sijn
def. Fut. Pret.	əi ʃəd bĭ sijĭŋ	əi ʃəd bĭ bĭjĭŋ sijn
Fut. Perf.	əi ʃl əv sijn	əi ʃl əv bĭjn sijn
def. Fut. Perf.	əi ʃl əv bĭjn sijĭŋ	əi ʃl əv bĭjn bĭjĭŋ sijn
	Conditional.	
Pres.	əi ʃəd sij	əi ʃəd bĭ sijn
def. Pres.	əi ʃəd bĭ sijĭŋ	əi ʃəd bĭ bĭjĭŋ sijn
Perf.	əi ʃəd əv sijn	əi ʃəd əv bĭjn sijn
def. Perf.	əi ʃəd əv bĭjn sijĭŋ	əi ʃəd əv bĭjn bĭjĭŋ sijn

	ACTIVE.	PASSIVE.
	Imperative.	
Pres.	sij (2 pers.)	bĭj sijn
	Infinitive.	
Pres.	tə sij	tə bĭ sijn
def. Pres.	tə bĭ sijĭŋ	tə bĭ bĭjĭŋ sijn
Perf.	tŭ əv sijn	tŭ əv bĭjn sijn
def. Perf.	tŭ əv bĭjn sijĭŋ	tŭ əv bĭjn bĭjĭŋ sijn
	Participle.	
Pres.	sijĭŋ	bĭjĭŋ sijn .
Pret.	———	sijn
Perf.	-hævĭŋ sijn	-hævĭŋ bĭjn sijn
def. Perf.	-hævĭŋ bĭjn sijĭŋ	-hævĭŋ bĭjn bĭjĭŋ sijn

Some of the longer forms—especially the definite tenses of the passive—seldom or never occur in speech.

For the subjunctive mood see p. 43.

The simple forms of the finite verb—pres., pret., and imper. —have special **emphatic** and **interrogative** forms compounded with *duw* 'do':

	Unemphatic.	*Emphatic.*	*Interrogative.*
Pres.	əi sij	əi ;duw sij	dŭw əi sij
Pret.	əi sɔ	əi ;did sij	dĭd əi sij
Imperf.	sij	;duw sij	——

The remaining emphatic forms are made simply by putting an emphatic stress on the auxiliary (of course in its strong form); the interrogative forms by transposing the pronoun and the auxiliary. As all the interrogative forms can also be made emphatic, we have in all eight forms. It will be enough to give those of the indef. pres. and fut. as examples:

Affirm. unemph.	əi sij	əi ʃl sij
Affirm. emph.	əi ·duw sij	əi ;ʃæl sij
Neg. unemph.	əi dount sij	əi ʃaant sij
Neg. emph.	əi ;dount sij	əi ;ʃaant sij
Aff. interr. unemph.	dŭw əi sij	ʃl əi sij
Aff. interr. emph.	;duw əi sij	;ʃæl əi sij
Neg. interr. unemph.	dount əi sij	ʃaant əi sij
Neg. interr. emph.	;dount əi sij	;ʃaant əi sij

In the Fut. and Cond. the first pers. only is formed with *ʃæl*, the others being formed with *wil*:

Sing.	1	əi ʃl sij	əi ʃəd sij
	2	jŭw l sij	jŭw d sij
	3	hĭj l (ʃĭjl, ĭtl) sij	hĭj d (ʃĭjd, ĭtəd) sij
Plur.	1	wĭj ʃl sij	wĭj ʃəd sij
	2	jŭw l sij	jŭw d sij
	3	-ðei l sij	-ðei d sij

This is the normal scheme, but it is subject to the following exceptions:

(*a*) In direct questions *ʃæl* is used instead of *wil* in the 2nd pers.: *jŭw l bĭ ðɛər əi sə:pouz* 'you will be there, I suppose', but *ʃl jŭ bĭ ðɛə'* 'shall you be there?'. In enclitic questions, however, a preceding *wud* is repeated: *jŭw l bí ðɛə :wount jŭ'* 'you will be there, will you not?'; *jŭw d þiŋk sŏu :wud nt jŭ'* 'you would think so, would you not?'

(*b*) After *if*, *an·les* and similar conjunctions all persons of the conditional are formed with *ʃud*: *əi wiʃ ĭj d kam* 'I wish he would come', but *:if ĭj ʃəd kam whəil əi m aut, aask* *ĭm tə weit* 'if he should come while I am out, ask him to wait'.

(*c*) Such combinations as *juw ənd ai*, *wij þrij*, *wĭj ɔl* 'you and I, we three, we all' take *wil* instead of *ʃæl*: *wij ʃl get -ðɛə fəəst* 'we shall get there first', but *əi ĭkspekt :juw ən ai əl get -ðɛə fəəst*; *wij þrij əl get -ðɛə fəəst.*

(*d*) *wil* or *ʃæl* can always be used to express the ideas of will or necessity in addition to that of pure futurity: *əi l kam əz suwn əz əi kæn* 'I will come as soon as I can'; *jŭw ʃl sij whŏt əi m :gouĭŋ tə duw* 'you shall see what I am going to do!' The emphatic *əi ;wil duw ĭt* expresses obstinacy, the emphatic *əi ;ʃæl duw ĭt* expresses determination.

Definite and Indefinite Tenses.

This important distinction is most clearly seen in the pres. While the def. pres. is strictly limited to what is actually going on at the moment of speaking, the indef. pres. includes past, present, and future, showing that an action or phenomenon is habitual or recurrent, or that a statement is of general application and holds good for all periods: *hĭj z ; aitĭŋ ə letə* implies therefore 'he is writing a letter at this moment', whilst *hĭj raits ə letə* almost excludes the idea of the actual present, and suggests some such complement as 'every day', 'now and then', to express the habit or repetition of the act of writing. Compare also *whɛər ə jŭ gouĭŋ*` 'where are you going?' with *hĭj gouz tə dʒəəmənĭ wans ə jiə* 'he goes to Germany once a year'.

But there are many verbs which generally occur only in the indefinite tenses. This is especially the case with verbs which express feelings, physical and mental perceptions, etc., such as *fijl*, *laik*, *þiŋk*: *əi :fijl il* 'I feel ill'; *hĭj laiks bĭjĭŋ hiə* 'he likes being here'; *ǝi þiŋk sǒu* 'I think so'. But as soon as the idea of volition or action becomes prominent, the definite tenses are employed: compare *ĭt hǝǝts* 'it hurts' with *hĭj z hǝǝtĭŋ ĭm* 'he is hurting him'; *hĭj daz nt sij ĭt* 'he does not see it' with *hĭj z sijĭŋ ðǝ saits* 'he is seeing the sights'; *ǝi :hiǝr ǝ noiz* 'I hear a noise' with *hĭj z hiǝrĭŋ lektʃǝz* 'he is hearing lectures'.

The distinction between the definite and indef. pret. is different. In the pres. the def. tense is absolute, the indef. relative; but in the pret. the indef. *ǝi rout ǝ letǝ jestǝdĭ* 'I wrote a letter yesterday' is absolute, whilst the def. *ǝi wǝz raitĭŋ ǝ letǝ jestǝdĭ* requires some such complement as 'when he came', to show that the action expressed by *wǝz raitĭŋ* has already occurred or continues during the action expressed by *:when ĭj keim*. In such examples as *wĭj wǝr ĭkspektĭŋ jŭ jestǝdĭ\ ; whai :did nt jŭ kam* 'we were expecting you yesterday; why did not you come?' the complementary indef. pret. is taken from the following sentence. The more absolutely the def. pret. is used, the more the idea of duration becomes prominent, as in *ǝi wǝz kɔfĭŋ ɔl :nait loŋ* 'I was coughing all night long', which is almost synonymous with *ǝi kɔft ɔl :nait loŋ ; wǝz kɔfĭŋ* however always implies an indef. pret. to be supplied in thought (such 'so that I could not sleep'), which *kɔft* is entirely absolute.

In the def. perf. and plup. the idea of duration is still more prominent: *:whot ǝv jŭ dan* 'what have you done?' means really 'what have you completed'; *:whot ǝv jŭ bĭjn duwĭŋ :ɔl :dei* 'what have you been doing all day?' on the contrary almost implies the idea of non-completion. There is the same distinction between *ǝi v þɔt ǝbǝut ĭt* 'I have thought about it' and *ǝi v bĭjn þiŋkiŋ ǝbǝut ĭt.*

The def. fut. *ǝi ʃl bĭ raitĭŋ* is quite analogous to the def. pres.

Perfect.

The perf. expresses a past occurrence whose consequences affect the immediate present: *əi v :kam tə sij jŭ* 'I have come to see you' (and am still here); *əi :keim tə sij jŭ* on the contrary implies that the speaker went away again; *əi v lɔst məi wotʃ* 'I have lost my watch', but *əi lɔst məi wotʃ jestədĭ, ən faund ĭt ə:gen* 'I lost my watch yesterday, and found it again'.

The use of the plup. is quite analogous.

Occasionally the perf. of intransitive verbs is formed with *iz* instead of *hæz: ĭz ĭj gon'* 'is he gone?' In such cases the partic. has almost the function of an adjective.

Future.

If an occurrence is clearly shown to be future by the context the pres. is used instead of the fut. and the perf. instead of the perf. fut. in dependent sentences: *ĭf jŭ duw ĭt, ĭt l bĭj əgenst ĭz wil* 'if you do it, it will be against his will'; *weit tĭl əi v finĭʃt məi letə* 'wait till I have finished my letter'. The fut. perf. only occurs in independent sentences: *əi ʃl əv finĭʃt məi letə bəi ðə taim jŏ redi* 'I shall have finished my letter by the time you are ready'. The simple pres. (or perf.) is used in independent sentences also in some cases where the sense of futurity is clear from the context: *hĭj staats fə ðə kontĭnənt təmorŏu* 'he starts for the Continent to-morrow.'

The fut. pres. has the same form as the conditional: *əi njuw :hau ĭt əd təən aut* 'I knew how it would turn out'.

The immediately impending ('on the point of..') is expressed by the definite tenses of *bĭj gouĭŋ: ĭt s :gouĭŋ tə rein* 'it is going to rain', *ĭt wəz :gouĭŋ tə rein*, etc.

əi m gouĭŋ, etc. by itself, like *əi m kamĭŋ* 'I am coming', has the meaning of an ordinary future: *əi m :gouĭŋ tə ðə þiətə tə:nait* 'I am going to the theatre to-night'; *when z ĭj :kamĭŋ bæk frəm əmerikə*` 'when is he coming back from America?'

Subjunctive.

The subj. hardly ever occurs except in combinations of *wəə* 'were' with *if*, and in expressions of wish formed with *wəə*: *:if ĭt wə posəbl* 'if it were possible'; *əi wiʃ ĭj wə gon* 'I wish he were gone'.

The pres. subj. only occurs in a few formal fossilized expressions of wish, such as *god :seiv ðə kwijn* 'God save the Queen!', *sou bij ĭt -ðen* 'so be it then!'.

Conditional.

The conditional is used in hypothetical sentences: *:if ĭj njuw ĭt, hĭj d tel mĭj ə:baut ĭt* 'if he knew it, he would tell me about it'; *:if ĭj d noun ĭt, hĭj d əv tould mĭj ə:baut ĭt* 'if he had known it, he would have told me about it'.

Also in sentences of wish: *əi wiʃ ĭj d kam* 'I wish he would come'. In chief sentences it expresses a modest wish or a request: *əi ʃəd laik tə :gou fər ə wɔk* 'I should like to go for a walk'; *əi ʃəd laik ə :glaas əv wɔtə* 'I should like a glass of water'.

ĭz tə sij.

This periphrasis serves chiefly to express necessity and possibility: *:when əm əi tə :kam əgen*` 'when am I to come again?'; *dount fəget jŏ tə bĭ ðɛər ĭgzæktlĭ ət faiv* 'do not forget you are to be there exactly at five'; *hĭj z not tə bĭ faund ;enĭwhɛə* 'he is not to be found anywhere'. In hypothetical sentences it expresses improbability: *:if wĭj wə* *tə mis ðə trein, ĭt əd bĭ raaðər ɔkwəd* 'if we were to miss the train, it would be rather awkward'.

Infinitive.

The infinitive is generally accompanied by *tŭ* ('supine'): *jŭw l hæv tə duw ĭt* 'you will have to do it'; *əi wont tə :gou houm* 'I want to go home'. The simple inf. only occurs after a few verbs, such as the defective *ʃæl*, etc., *let*, *sij*, *fijl* and others that express physical or mental perceptions: *let ĭm gou* 'let him go'; *əi sɔ ĭm :gou aut* 'I saw him go out'.

The supine is used in a passive sense in some formal phrases: *ðə z ə haus tə :let ĭn ðis strijt* 'there is a house to let in this street'.

Participles and Gerund.

The pres. part. is sometimes used in a passive sense: *ðə z ən aansə :weitĭŋ* 'there is an answer waiting'.

The pres. part. serves as a gerund, that is, a form intermediate between verb and abstract noun, which combines the syntactical peculiarities of both parts of speech, as in the following examples: *ðə z nou :getĭŋ rid əv ĭm* 'there is no getting rid of him'; *əi rĭmembə sijĭŋ ĭm* 'I remember seeing him'; *əi :hæv nt ðə :plegər əv nouĭŋ ĭm* 'I have not the pleasure of knowing him'; *hĭj ĭnsistĭd ŏn məi stopĭŋ ðə nait* 'he insisted on my stopping the night'.

TEXTS.

ðə san.

ðə san sez :

məi neim z ·san. əi m verĭ brait.

əi raiz ĭn ðĭ ijst ; ən :when əi :raiz, ĭt s dei.

əi luk in ət jŏ windŏu wĭð məi brait, gouldn ai, ən tel jŭ :when ĭt s taim tə -get ap ; ənd əi :sei ' ·slagəd, -get ·ap ' ; əi dount ʃain fə jŭ tə :lai ĭn bed ən slijp, bət əi ʃain fə jŭ tə -get ap ən wəək \, ən rijd \, ən :wɔk əbaut \.

əi m ə :greit trævl-ə : əi :trævl ɔl ŏuvə ðə :skai ; əi nevə stop, ənd əi m nevə taiəd.

əi v ə ·kraun ŏn məi :hed \, ə kraun əv brait reiz \, ənd əi send əut məi :reiz ·evrĭwhɛə. əi :ʃain ŏn ðə trijz, ən ðə hauzĭz, ən ðə wɔtə ; ənd evrĭþĭŋ :luks spaaklĭŋ ən bjuwtĭfl -when əi ʃain ŏn ĭt.

əi :giv jŭ lait ; ənd əi :giv jŭ hijt \, fər əi :meik evrĭþĭŋ wɔm. əi :meik ðə ·fruwt raipn, ənd əi :meik ðə ·kɔn raipn. :if əi did nt ʃain ŏn ðə fijldz ən gaadnz, naþĭŋ əd grou.

əi m verĭ :hai ap ĭn ðə skai \, haiə ðən ɔl ðə trijz \, haiə ðən ðə klaudz \, haiə ðən ·evrĭþĭŋ : əi m ə greit -wei ɔf.

:if əi wə tə -kam niərə t jŭ, əi ʃəd skɔtʃ jŭ tə deþ \, ənd əi ʃəd bəən -ap ðə graas \, fər əi m ɔl meid əv hot, glouĭŋ faiə.

əi v :bijn ĭn ðə skai ə loŋ taim \—loŋgə ðən ·enĭwan kən rĭmembə ; bət əi v not :groun ould :jet.

samtəimz əi teik -ɔf məi kraun əv brait reiz, ən ræp -ap məi hed ĭn þin silvə klaudz; ən ðen jŭ kən luk ət mĭ; bət :when ðər ə nou :klaudz, ənd əi :ʃain wĭð ɔl məi :braitnĭs ət nuwn, jŭ ·kaant :luk ət mĭ\`, fər əi ʃəd dæzl jŏr aiz ən :meik jŭ blaind. ðĭ ·ijgl z ðĭ ounlĭ :krijtʃə ðət kən :luk ət mĭj :ðen : ðĭ ijgl wĭð ĭz stroŋ, piəsĭŋ ai kən ɔlwĭz :luk ət mĭj.

:when əi m gŏuĭŋ tə raiz ĭn ðə mɔnĭŋ tə :meik ĭt dei, ðə laaks :flai ap ĭn ðə skai tə mijt mĭ\`, ən siŋ swijtlĭ ĭn ðĭ ɛə; ən ðə kok krouz laud tə tel evrĭbodĭ əi m kamĭŋ; bət ðĭ aulz ən ðə bæts :flai əwei :when -ðei sij mĭ\`, ən haid ðəm-selvz ĭn ould wɔlz ən holŏu trijz; ən ðə laiənz ən taigəz :gou ĭntə -ðɛə denz ən keivz ən slijp -ðɛər ɔl ðə dei.

əi :ʃain ĭn ɔl :pleisĭz: əi :ʃain ĭn iŋglənd, ənd ĭn fraans, ənd ĭn dʒəəmənĭ, ənd ɔl ŏuvə ðĭ əəþ.

əi m ðə :mous(t) bjuwtĭfl ən glɔrĭəs :krijtʃə ðət kən bĭ sijn ĭn ðə houl wəəld.

ðə muwn.

ðə muwn sez:

məi neim z ·muwn; əi ʃain tə :giv jŭ lait ət nait\`, -when ðə san z set.

əi m verĭ bjuwtĭfl, ən whait ləik silvə.

jŭw kən luk ət mĭj when·evə jŭ laik\`, fər əi m not sŏu brait əz tə dæzl jŏr aiz\`, ənd əi nevə skɔtʃ jŭ. əi m maild ən dʒentl. əi :let ijvn ðə :litl ·glouwəəmz :ʃain; ən ðɛə kwait daak bəi dei.

ðə staaz :ʃain -ɔl raund mĭ, bət əi m bigər ən braitə ðən eni ə ðəm; ənd əi :luk ləik ə big pəəl ə:maŋ smɔl, spaaklĭŋ daiəməndz.

:when jŏr əslijp, əi ʃain þrŭw ðə kəətnz wĭð məi dʒentl reiz; ənd əi sei ‘slijp on: əi wount dĭstəəb jŭ.’

. ðə naitĭŋgeil siŋz tə mĭj‵, ən ʃĭj :siŋz betə ðən ɔl ðĭ -aðə :bəədz :put təgeðə. ʃĭj :sits ĭn ə þɔnbuʃ, ən :siŋz mĭloudjəslĭ ɔl :nait loŋ‵, :whail ðə djuw :laiz ŏn ðə graas, ən evrĭþĭŋ z kwaiət ən sailənt ɔl raund.

rein.

rein :kamz frəm ðə klaudz.

luk ət ðŏuz blæk klaudz! həu faast -ðei :muwv əloŋ! nau -ðei v hidn ðe san. -ðei v :kavəd ĭt ap dʒast əz jŭ kavər -ap jŏ feis -when jŭ :þrou ə hæŋkətʃĭf ŏuvər ĭt. ðə z ə litl bĭt əv bluw skai stil. nau ðə z nou :bluw :skai ətɔl: ĭt s ɔl blæk wĭð ðə klaudz. ĭt s verĭ daak‵, ləik nait.

ĭt l rein :suwn. ·nau ĭt s bĭ:ginĭŋ tə rein. :whot big drops! ðə daks ə :verĭ glæd‵, bət ðə litl bəədz ə not :glæd: -ðei :gou ən ʃeltə ðəm-selvz -andə ðə bauz ə ðə trijz.

nau ðə :rein z ouvə. ĭt wəz ^ounlĭ ə ʃauə. nau ðə flauəz :smel swijt‵, ən ðə san ʃainz‵, ən ðə litl bəədz siŋ ə:gen‵, ənd ĭt s not sŏu hot əz ĭt :woz bi:fɔr ĭt reind.

ðə kauədlĭ :litl boi.

ðə wəz wans ə :litl boi‵, hŭ wəz ə greit kauəd. hĭj wəz ə:freid əv :ɔlmŏust evrĭþĭŋ. hĭj wəz əfreid ə ðə tuw kidz‵, nænĭ ən bilĭ‵, :when -ðei :keim ən :put -ðɛə nouzĭz þrŭw ðə peilĭŋz ĭn ðə jaad: hĭj wəz əfreid tə pul bilĭz biəd. :whot ə silĭ :litl boi ĭj woz! whot wəz ĭz neim‵? nou‵, əi ʃaan :tel ĭz neim‵, fər əi m ə·ʃeimd əv ĭm.

wel\`, ĭj wəz verĭ -matʃ ə:freid əv dogz :tuw ; hĭj ɔlwĭz kraid ĭf ĭj həəd ə :dog baak\`, ən :ræn əwei ən tuk :hould əv ĭz maðəz eiprən ləik ə beibĭ. :whot ə silĭ :felŏu ĭj woz ! fə dogz dount həət jŭ :nou : -ðɛə ·fond əv :litl boiz\`, ən :laik tə plei wĭ ðəm. dĭd jŭ evə :sij ə dog ijt ap ə :litl boi ? nou\`, nevə\`, ai m :ʃuə.

wel\`— sŏu ðĭs silĭ :litl boi wəz :wɔkĭŋ bəi ĭmself :wan :dei, ənd ə pritĭ blæk dog :keim aut əv ə haus, ən :sed ' :bau wau ' ; ən keim tŭ ĭm\`, ən :wontĭd tə plei wĭð ĭm ; bət ðə :litl boi :ræn əwei. ðə dog :ræn aaftər ĭm, ən baakt laudə ' bau wau ' ; bət ĭj ounlĭ :ment tə sei ' :gud mɔnĭŋ\`, hau djŭ duw\` ? ' bət ðə :litl boi wəz terəblĭ fraitnd\`, ən ræn əwei əz faast əz ĭj kud\`, wĭðaut :lukĭŋ bĭfɔr ĭm ; ənd ĭj tambld ĭntŭ ə madĭ ditʃ\`, ən ðɛr ĭj :lei kraiĭŋ ət ðə botəm ə ðə ditʃ\`, fər ĭj kudnt -get aut.

ənd əi riəlĭ bĭlijv ĭj d əv lein -ðɛər ɔl dei, bət ðə dog wəz sou gud·neitʃəd ðət ĭj went tə ðə haus -whɛə ðə litl :boi livd ŏn pəəpəs tə tel ðəm whɛər ĭj woz. sŏu :when ĭj :keim tə ðə haus, hĭj skrætʃt ət ðə dɔə\`, ən :sed ' :bau wau'; fər ĭj kud n't spijk -enĭ pleinə. sŏu -ðei oupnd ðə dɔr ən :sed ' :who də jŭ wont\`, jŭ blæk dog\` ? : wĭj dount nou jŭ.' :ðen ðə dog went tə rælf ðə mæn, ən puld ĭm bəi ðə kout\`, ən puld ət ĭm tĭl ĭj brɔt ĭm tə ðə ditʃ ; ən ðə dog ən rælf təgeðə :got ðə :litl boi aut ə ðə ditʃ ; bət ĭj wəz ɔl ŏuvə mad, ən kwait wet ; ən evrĭbŏdĭ laaft ət ĭm fə :bijĭŋ sətʃ ə kauəd.

ðĭ aidl boi.

ðə wəz wans ə :litl boi ; hĭj woz nt ə ·big :boi\`, fər if ĭj d bĭjn ə big :boi, əi səpouz ĭj d əv bĭjn waizə ; hĭj wəz ounlĭ ə litl :boi\`, nou haiə ðən :ðis teibl\`, ənd ĭz faaðər ən maðə sent ĭm tə skuwl.

ĭt wəz ə verĭ :pleznt mɔnĭŋ : ðə san ʃon, ən ðə bəədz sæŋ ĭn ðə trijz. :nau ðĭs :litl boi did nt ·kεə :matʃ fər ĭz buks ˎ, fər ĭj wəz ə silĭ :litl boi ˎ, əz əi tould jŭ ; ənd ĭj þɔt ĭj d raaðə plei ðən :gou tə skuwl.

ənd ĭj :sɔ ə ·bij -flaiĭŋ ɔ:baut, fəəst tə ·wan :flauə, ən ðen tŭ ənaðə. sŏu ĭj :sed ' pritĭ bij, :wil jŭ :kam ən plei wĭð mĭj ? ' bət ðə bij :sed ' ^nou, əi mas nt bĭ aidl : əi məs :gou ən :gæðə hanĭ.'

:ðen ĭj :met ə dog ˎ, ənd ĭj :sed ' dog, :wil jŭ plei wĭð mĭj ? ' bət ðə dog :sed ' ^nou, əi mas nt bĭ aidl : əim :gouĭŋ tə :kætʃ ə hεə fə məi maastəz dinə ; ei məs :meik heist ən kætʃ ĭt.'

:ðen ðə :litl boi paast bəi ə ·heirik ˎ, ənd ĭj :sɔ ə bəəd pulĭŋ səm hei :aut ə ðə heirik ˎ, ənd ĭj :sed ' bəəd, :wil jŭ :kam ən plei wĭð mĭj ? ' bət ðə bəəd :sed ' ^nou, əi mas nt bĭj aidl : əi məs -get səm hei tə :bild məi nest wĭð ˎ, ən səm mos ˎ, ən səm wul.' sŏu ðə bəəd :fluw əwei.

:ðen ðə :litl boi :sɔ ə ·hɔs ˎ, ən :sed ' hɔs, :wil jŭ plei wĭð mĭj ? ' bət ðə hɔs :sed ' ^nou, əi mas nt bĭj aidl : əi məs :gou ən plau ˎ, ŏə ðə wount bĭj -enĭ kɔn tə :meik bred ŏv.'

ðen ðə :litl boi sed tŭ ĭm-self ' whot ˊ ! ĭz ·noubədi aidl ? ðen :litl ·boiz :mas nt bĭj :aidl aiðə.' sŏu ĭj :meid heist ən :went tə skuwl ˎ, ən ləənt ĭz lesnz verĭ wel ˎ, ən ðə maastə :sed ĭj wəz ə verĭ :gud boi.

ðĭ ould tʃæpl.

ĭt s mɔə ðən ·twentĭ :jiəz əgou ˎ, ən :jet əi rĭmembər ĭt əz :if ĭt wə ·jestədĭ ˎ—ðə brait dʒuwn mɔnĭŋ ai ən :tuw aðə :boiz, ned tanstl ən hærĭ web, :sæt ət ðə raitĭŋdesk ĭn əuə skuwlrum. wĭj :hæd ðə skuwlrum ɔl tə əuə:selvz ˎ, fə ðə maastər ən ðĭ aðə :boiz hæd nt :kam in -jet. əi rĭmembə həu ðə sanʃain :keim strijmĭŋ in ŏuvə -ðæt ould desk. həu :hækt əbaut ĭt wŏz', ən steind wĭð iŋk! ən nou wandə: fə menĭ dʒenə·reiʃənz əv boiz əd :kat -ðɛər ĭniʃəlz ŏn ĭt', ən dæmĭdʒd ĭt əut əv pjuə mistʃĭf. əi rĭmembə həu ðə tʃiəfl lait :meid əs :luk ap', ən həu brait, ən bluw, ən træns·pɛərənt ðə skai lukt þrŭw ðĭ oupn windŏu; ənd :hau ðə soŋ ə ðə bəədz ən ðə freʃ kantrĭ oudəz :keim pɔrĭŋ in frəm ðə fijldz bi:fɔə ðə haus; ənd əi rĭmembə həu ned tanstl :təənd ĭz stroŋ, radĭ fijtʃəz tɔdz əs ən :sed 'ou :whot ə dei ðĭs əd :bij fə ðĭ ould tʃæpl!'

ət ðə menʃən ə ðĭ ould tʃæpl hærĭ :web ən ai dʒampt ap ən ĭkskleimd 'whot ə dei! :if wĭj wər ounlĭ ðɛə!'

wij :þrij boiz wə pjuwplz əv ðə vikər əv heizfəd; hærĭ web wəz ĭz san. ðə wər ɔltə·geðər ə:baut haafədazn boiz ĭn ðə skuwl. -ðei wə ðə sanz əv ĭz :moust weltəduw pəriʃənəz. ðə wəəðĭ vikə hæd nt ə :laadʒ iŋkam; ənd ĭj dĭvoutĭd ðə houl əv ĭz :liʒə taim tŭ əs. ned tanstl wəz ðə san əv ə faamər ŭw :livd tuw :mailz ɔf; ən ðĭ ould tʃæpl wəz ə:baut faiv mailz ŏn ðĭ aðə said əv :ðɛə faam. ned wəz ə:baut twelv', bət ĭj wəz sou stroŋlĭ bilt, ənd :hæd sətʃ stroŋ bould fijtʃəz ðət ĭj :lukt sam :jiəz ouldə. hĭz bodĭ ən maind wə bouþ ful əv raf streŋþ ən helþĭ enədʒĭ. hĭj pleid ĭz :paat mænfl-ĭ ət ðə dinəteibl əz :wel əz ĭn ðə pleigraund. hĭj wəz ə dɛərĭŋ, əbstrepərəs, ouvə·bɛərĭŋ :boi. hĭj wəz gud ət ɔl autdɔə geimz n spɔts'—ranĭŋ, dʒampĭŋ, lijpĭŋ wi ðə poul, reslĭŋ, swimĭŋ'—ən :went in fə ðəm wĭð ə vigər ən ĭnþjuwzĭæzm ðət :fild əs ɔl wĭð wandə. ən ĭj -hæd ə kɔs, houmlĭ, konfĭdenʃəl kəind əv eləkwəns ɔl əbəut dogz, kæts, ræbĭts, pidʒənʃuwtĭŋ, bəədz-nestĭŋ, ən wijzlhantĭŋ wĭð ĭz raf :grei teriə ·snæp. samtəimz ĭj :juws(t) tə tel əs əv ĭz ekspĭ·diʃənz þrŭw ðə wudz ən fijldz :raund ĭz houm', ənd həu ĭj ĭksplɔd ðə solĭtərĭ bruks ən pondz; ən :ðen ĭjd diskraib ðə kjuəriəs ænĭmlz ən bəədz ĭj :sɔˋ— otəzˋ, bædʒəzˋ, poulkætsˋ, hɔksˋ, dʒeizˋ, ən :nou end əv aðə streinʒ krijtʃəz. ɔl ðis ĭj dĭ:skraibd sou vivĭdlĭ ən ĭn -satʃ ə fæsĭneitĭŋ stail ðət ĭj bĭ:keim ðə greit orĭkl ə ðə skuwl ŏn ɔl ðə wandəz ə ðə kantrĭ; ən wĭj lisnd tŭ ĭm tĭl əuə hedz wə təəndˋ, ənd əuə maindz wə fild wĭð ɔl :sɔts əv skijmz əv ədventʃə.

wel, hĭj d tɔkt ouvər ən ouvər əgen əv ðis ould tʃæpl tĭl wĭj wə mæd tə gou -ðɛə. ĭt wəz ə ruwĭnd tʃæpl; ĭt :lei ĭn ə dijp ən solĭtrĭ vælĭ. ə:kɔdĭŋ tə him ĭt woz nt ə :pleis tə vizĭt bəi nait: hĭj wud nt gou -ðɛə bəi nait fə ðə ·wəəld, ĭj :sed. ĭt wəz hɔntĭd bəi ə və:raiĭtĭ əv mĭstiərĭəs gousts; ən bĭsaidz, :sevrəl ·məədəz əd bĭjn kəmitĭd -ðɛə, ənd aðə :horəz. bət bəi deiləit ənd ĭn samə, ə:kɔdĭŋ tə hiz dĭskripʃən, ĭt wəz ə pəəfĭkt ·pærədəis fə boiz. ðə wə ·poulkæts ĭn ðə ruwĭnz; ən -sam ə ðə rɛərĭst kəindz əv bəədz :bilt ĭn ðĭ ould mosĭ trijz. ðə wə dʒeiz :nests, raineks n staalĭŋz :nests; ðə feðə-pouk :bilt ĭz bjuwtĭfl :litl kavəd nests -ðɛə; ðə wər ijvn ·kukŭwz :egz tə bĭ faund -ðɛə; ən ĭn ðə lɔft ə ðĭ ould tʃæpl ðə wə :lots əv aulz.

wəz ðər evər ə :boi ĭn ðə wəəld ŭw kəd hiər əv sətʃ ə :pleis wĭð:aut loŋĭŋ tə bĭ ɔf tŭ ĭt? wĭj d lisnd sŏu ɔfn tə nedz əkaunt əv ĭts wandəz, ðət nau, ət ðə :miə menʃən ŏv ĭt, wĭj dʒampt ap ən :sed 'whot ə pleis! ən whot weðə! ned! ned! whot ʃəl wĭj duwˋ?' 'ˇai nou', sĭd ned; hĭj dʒampt ap ŏn ðĭ opəzĭt :said ə ðə desk, ən lent ouvə -tɔdz əs, ən :lukt :verĭ ĭmpɔtnt; :ðen ĭj :went onˋ 'ĭt s fain tə:dei, ən ĭt l bĭ fain təmorŏu tuwˋ— ðə weðər əl bĭ setld fə sam taim. əuə ʃepəd :sez sŏuˋ, ən hij nouz. ən təmorŏu z ·þəəzdĭ, ən wĭj -hæv ə haaf holĭdĭ. wĭj v ounlĭ :got tŭ aask lijv fə juw tə -kam ən sij mĭj, ən ðə þiŋz dan.' wĭj bouþ :sed 'jesˋ, jesˋ, -ðæt əd bĭ glɔrĭəs; bət ·wil mĭstə web :let əs gouˋ?' ned :sed 'lijv

-ðæt tə mij: ai l mænĭdʒ ĭt. əi l sei məi faaðər ən maðə wont jŭw tə :gou ən sij ðəm fər ə houl dei‛— ən :sou -ðei duw‛, fə -ðei v ɔfn sed sŏu; ənd əi ·nou mĭstə web :wount rĭfjuwz əs -ðen. ·wij l duw ĭt, məi boiz, ·wij l duw ĭt!' ənd ət ðə :miə þɔt əv ĭt wĭj dramd ŏn ðə :desk wĭð əuə fists, ən daanst əbaut tĭl wĭj nokt ŏuvə ðə fɔmz bĭhaind əs‛, sŏu ðət ðe noiz wouk :ap əuə revrənd prĭseptə ĭn ĭz ijzĭ tʃɛə‛, ən wij həəd ðə dɔr oupn, ənd -hæd haadlĭ :taim tə :put ðə fɔmz :ap ə:gen, si daun, en :luk siəriəs bĭ:fɔr ĭj keim in.

əi nijd nt sei hau wĭj dĭd əuə lesnz -ðæt :dei. ðə houl taim əuə hedz wə ful əv ould tʃæplz, aulz :nests, kukŭwz :egz ənd aðə treʒəz ə ðə seim kaind; ənd if wĭj ĭskeipt bĭjĭŋ noutĭst ən panĭʃt, ĭt wəz ounlĭ bĭ:koz mĭstə web wəz əwei ət ə wedĭŋ ŏ fjuwnərəl moust ə ðə :taim. əz :suwn əz :skuwl wəz ouvə, tanstl :keim ap tŭ ĭm wĭð ĭz hæt ĭn ĭz hænd, ən :aast lijv fŏr əs ĭn ðə :neim əv ĭz pɛərənts. :mistə web :lukt :raaðə greiv, ən :sijmd tə bĭ þiŋkĭŋ ðə -mætər ouvə. wĭj :felt æŋʃəs‛, ənd əuə haats :sæŋk lou. bət :when ĭj d aast ned ə :fjuw pətikjələz, ĭj lukt ap, ən :sed 'wel, ðə weðə z səətnlĭ :verĭ fain‛, ənd əi riəli þiŋk ĭt l :duw jŭ gud; sŏu əi wount :sei noŭ, ĭf midltənz pɛərənts hæv nt -enĭ əbdʒekʃən; bət maind jŭ kijp əut əv mistʃif‛, ən kam bæk ĭn gud taim.' əv :kɔs wĭj promĭst mŏust librəlĭ‛, ən left ðə skuwl verĭ kwaiətlĭ, til wĭjd wɔkt sam wei, ən :got ŏn ðĭ aðə :said əv ə baan; ən :ðen wĭj let ɔf ðə stijm bəi daansĭŋ, ʃautĭŋ, ən klæpĭŋ hændz ɔl təgeðə.

:ai əd nou -greit difĭkltĭ ĭn :getĭŋ lijv frəm məi pɛərənts tə -gŏu ən :sij ned, :when -ðei njuw ðət hærĭ webz faaðər əd əlaud him tə :gou tuw‛, ənd ŏn ðĭ andəstændĭŋ ðət ĭt wəz ət ðə dĭzaiər əv nedz pɛərənts; bət əi faund ĭt wəz not sŏu ijzĭ tŭ ə:pijz məi konʃəns əbəut ðə :mætə. əi traid tə :meik þĭŋz ijzĭ bəi seiĭŋ tə məi-self ðət nedz pɛərənts ·did :wont əs tə :gou. bət ðə konʃəns ĭz nætʃərəlĭ sensĭtĭv ĭn əəlĭ juwþ‛, ən main əd bĭjn tendəlĭ delt wĭð bəi məi pɛərənts\`, ənd ĭt ʃoud mĭj əz kliəlĭ əz posəbl ðət ðə wəz beisnĭs ən dĭsepʃən ĭn ðə houl mænər əv :getĭŋ lijv fə ðis vizĭt. ĭt :sijmd tə sei '·when dĭd nedz pɛərənts aask jŭ\` ? :if evə, səətnlĭ :not :dʒes nau. ən jet ðis ĭz :whot jŭ :wont jŏ pɛərənts ən jŏ maastə tə bĭlijv\`, :ðou jŭ dount ĭg:zæktlĭ sei ĭt. bĭsaidz\`, jŭ prĭtend jŏ :gouĭŋ tə nedz pɛərənts, when jŏ ·riəlĭ :gouĭŋ tə ðĭ ould tʃæpl. ĭt s ə bæd biznĭs'. əi traid tŭ ĭveid ðis kliə demən·streiʃən\`, ən :traid tə stop məi iəz tə ðə vois əv konʃəns ; bət ĭt wəz ĭn vein: ə sens əv ijvl ən kondĭm·neiʃən rĭmeind :ijvn -aaftə ðə vois wəz sailənt.

bət monĭŋ keim, ənd əi wouk ap ; ðə san wəz porĭŋ in ə flad əv lait : əi dʒampt ap ; ət fəəst əi -hæd ə :fijlĭŋ əv sædnĭs\`, ənd əi said -when əi rĭmembəd :hau əi d :dʒoind ĭn roŋduwĭŋ ən dĭsijt ; bət :when əi :lukt aut ən :sɔ ðə glorĭ ən bjuwtĭ əv ðə monĭŋ'— :when əi :sɔ ðə waid fijldz stijmĭŋ ĭn ðə monĭŋ san'— :sɔ ðə trijz ən buʃĭz weivĭŋ ĭn ðə lait brijz'— :sɔ ðə kliə skai, ən həəd ðə bəədz :siŋĭŋ ræptʃərəslĭ ɔl raund, əi :felt satʃ dĭlait ət ðə prospĭkt əv ðə dei bĭfɔr əs ðət əi fəgot ɔl məi skruwplz\`, ən raʃt :daun stɛəz, swolŏud məi brekfəst, ən harĭd ɔf tə mijt hærĭ web. hærĭ web wəz kwait əz ĭksaitĭd əz ai wŏz ; bət :when əi :lukt ĭn ĭz feis, wĭð ĭts peil, delĭkĭt fijtʃəz, əi þɔt əi kəd :sij treisĭz əv ðə seim mentl straglz ðət ·ai d :gɔn þruw ; fə hærĭ web wəz ə :boi əv ə timĭd ən dʒentl dispə·ziʃən ; hĭj wəz ijzl-ĭ :led ĭntə mistʃĭf, bət dʒest əz ijzl-ĭ fraitnd ət deindʒə ŏ ðə þɔt əv :duwĭŋ roŋ. həuevə, wĭj didnt :stop tə tɔk əv əuə fijlĭŋz\`, bət set ɔf fə nedz haus.

ĭf evə ðə wəz ə :dei əv splendə, ən bjuwtĭ, ən dʒoi, ĭt wəz ðæt :dei. ĭt wəz :niə ðĭ :end əv dʒuwn ; ðə fouljĭdʒ wəz ĭn ĭts atməst lag·ʒuəriəns ; ðə skai wəz ɔl wan delĭkĭt træns·pɛərənt bluw ; ðə fijldz wə ful əv flauɔrĭŋ, sentĭd graasĭz, redĭ tə bĭ moun; waild rouzĭz ən eldəflauəz weivd ĭn ðə brijzĭ hedʒrouz ˋ, ən :spred -ðɛə freigrənṣ faar ən waid; ðə laak wəz :hovərĭŋ ĭn ðĭ :ɛə; ðə kukŭw flitĭd frəm pleis to pleis ˋ, ənd atəd ĭts dijpĭst ən melŏuĭst nouts; ðə graashopə tʃəəpt ĭn ðə təəf ət əuə fijt ˋ, ən þauzndz əv insekts hamd əraund əs ˋ— þauzndz əv :krijtʃəz :atərĭŋ voisĭz əv dĭlait.

enĭwan ŭw nouz ˊ— ən huw daznt :nou ˋ? — həu ful əv glædnĭs ən bjuwtĭ ən wandə ɔl krĭ:eiʃən :iz tŭ ə tʃaild, həu :litl -ðei :nou əv fiər ŏr æŋ·zaiĭtĭ, nevə :stopĭŋ tə rĭflekt ŏn ðə swift :paasĭŋ əwei əv ɔl əuər ĭndʒoimənts, bət :spredĭŋ -ðɛə houl haat ən houp ŏuvə ðə houl fɛərĭlænd həraizn əraund ðəm ˊ— enĭwan ŭw :nouz ɔl ðis, wĭl ges wĭð :whot egzal·teiʃən wĭj got -ɔf ðə dastĭ roud, ən skauəd əlŏŋ ðə paaðz þrŭw ðə freʃ medŏuz ŏn əuə :wei tə nedz haus; :hau wĭj ræn ĭntə ðə dijp graas ap tŭ əuə weists ˋ, when:evə wĭj :sɔ ə laak raiz ŏ :flai daun ˋ, ĭn ðə houp əv faindĭŋ ðə nest; ən :ðen :ræn on, pijpĭŋ ĭntŭ :evrĭ buʃ ən bæŋk, siŋĭŋ -sam skuwlboi soŋ tə rĭ:lijv əuə haats əv ðə bəədn əv dʒoi.

wĭj suwn -kɔt :sait əv ned sitĭŋ ŏn ə geit, :lukĭŋ aut fər əs; ðə moumĭnt ĭj sɔ əs, ĭj dʒamt daun, ən -keim :ranĭŋ tə mijt əs wĭð ĭz grei terĭə ət ĭz hijlz. ən nau wĭj ɔl þrij :set ɔf fə ðĭ ould tʃæpl əz hæpĭ əz kəd bij. wĭj d fəgotn ɔl əbəut əuə konʃənsĭz. :æz fə ned, əi daut ĭf ĭj d evə -givn ðə :mætər ə þɔt ˋ, :ijvn ət ðə bĭginĭŋ. wĭj wər əz hæpĭ əz enĭ :krijtʃəz ŏn əəþ ·kud bij. wĭj -æd ðə :sens əv pəəfĭkt libətĭ; wĭj -æd ə houl samə dei bĭfɔr əs ˋ, whĭtʃ tŭ ə boi iz ən ĭ·təənĭtĭ; ðə wər :obdʒĭkts əv ĭngrousĭŋ intərest ɔl raund əs; ən sou wĭj :went on ˋ, lukĭŋ ĭntŭ evrĭþĭŋ, laafĭŋ, wandrĭŋ evrĭ step əv əuə faiv :mail dʒəənĭ. tŭ ə ·mæn faiv mailz ĭz ·naþĭŋ; tŭ ə ·boi ĭt s ə :dʒəənĭ əv vaast mægnĭtjŭwd ˋ, :fild wĭð ĭm:preʃənz ðət l nevə bĭ fəgotn.

ðə :kantrĭ wĭj paast þrŭw ˊ— əz ai rĭmembər ĭt ˊ— stil

sijmz tə mĭj wandəfl-ĭ bjuwtĭfl. ned tanstl :sijmd tŭ əs ðə :moust nouĭŋ əv mɔtlz. hĭj nau bĭ-gæn tə ʃou əs whŏt ĭj kəd duw\`, ən pruwv ðət ĭj hædnt boustĭd fə naþĭŋ. wĭj :həəd ĭz dog baakĭŋ laudlĭ\`, ən ræn tə ðə :pleis əz kwik əz wĭj kud\`, ən sɔ ĭm — wĭð ə long ·sneik ĭn ĭz :mauþ\`, ən ʃeikĭŋ ĭt fjuərĭəslĭ\`, whəil ĭt raiðd ĭn ĭz dʒɔz\`, ən sent aut ə mŏust panʒənt ən venəməs smel. ðə dog suwn kild ĭt\`, ən ned tuk əut ĭz naif, ən stript -ɔf ĭts skin\`, ən held ĭt ap tŭ :auər ədmaiərĭŋ aiz: ĭt :lukt ləik ə bjuwtĭfl vɛərĭgeitĭd ribən. bət ðis :woz nt ɔl: hĭj :kat ĭt oupn, ən wĭj :sɔ tŭ əuər əstonĭʃmənt ə hjuwdʒ toud ðət ĭt əd swolŏud houl. wĭj went on, :fild wĭð wandər ət ðĭjz njuw ən streinʒ fækts. ned rouz :nou end ĭn əuər estĭ·meiʃən.

ðə nekst moumĭnt wĭj əgen :həəd ðə dog baak\`, ən :when wĭj :keim ap tŭ ĭm, wĭj :faund ĭm wĭð ə priklĭ bɔl\`, niəlĭ əz big əz :wan əv əuə hedz\`, :roulĭŋ ĭt əbaut; hĭjd :faund ĭt ĭn ə hijp əv ded lijvz ət ðə :botəm əv ə ditʃ. ned wəz dĭlaitĭd\`, ən kraid aut 'ə hedʒog\`, ə hedʒog'. :ðen ĭj :sed 'ʃəl mai dog kil ĭt? ĭt :iz nt ^evrĭ :dog ðət kən :kil ə :hedʒog. ᵛmain kæn: :let ĭm əloun ə :minĭt\`, ən juw l :suwn sij'. wĭj :sed 'nou\`, nou\`, :let ðə puə þĭŋ liv'. ':veri wel\`' sĭd ned. hĭj puld ĭz :dog ɔf, ən wĭj :went ən :stud ə :litl -wei ɔf, ən tŭ əuə wandər ən dĭlait :suwn :sɔ ðə :priklĭ :bɔl kɔʃəslĭ an·roul, ən grædʒŭəlĭ :put fɔþ ə blæk snaut ən fɔə blæk, ʃainĭŋ legz\`, ən skæmpər əwei ĭntə ðə hedʒ.

:whail wĭj wə ful əv ðĭs :sijn, ðə sadnlĭ -keim :swijpĭŋ raund əs səm bəədz wĭð laadʒ wiŋz, ən atərĭŋ ʃril, waild kraiz. :samtəimz -ðei rouz ĭntə ðĭ ɛə wĭð ə weivərĭŋ flait\`, :samtəimz -ðei :pitʃt hevĭlĭ daun\`, ən :ðen :fluw ap ə-gen\`, whijlĭŋ hiər ən ðɛə\`, ən :sijmd əz :if -ðei wə gŏuĭŋ tə :flai əwei frəm əs, -when :ɔl əv ə sadn -ðei :keim bæk əz kwiklĭ əz -ðei d gɔn, ən defnd əs wĭð -ðɛə meləŋkəlĭ læmĭn·teiʃənz. :samtəimz

-ðei :dæʃt klous bai əs wĭð laud loŋdrən ʃrijks ən tŭwuwz ', əz :if -ðei wə mæd wĭð grijf ən terə. 'wĭj d betə :kijp ə ʃaap luk·aut -hiə ' ', -sed ned ', 'ðĭ egz ə ðĭjz pijwĭts kaant bĭ faar ɔf '— ŏ præps ðə jaŋ bəədz '. ĭn ənaðə minĭt ĭj stopt, ən pointĭd ət ðə graund '— ə :pijs əv bɛə paastʃə. wĭj kəd :sij naþĭŋ bət səm daaklukĭŋ :þiŋz ləik lamps əv braun klei ', ən aast ĭm whot -ðei wəə. ':whai -ðɛə jaŋ ^pijwĭts ' ', ĭj :sed; ən :ðou -ðei :lei əz mouʃənlĭs əz :if -ðei wə ·riəlĭ :lamps əv :klei, hĭj put ðəm ĭn ən emtĭ ·blækbəədz :nest, ən maatʃt ɔf wĭ ðəm. tə kənvins əs ðət -ðei ·wəə nt :riəlĭ ded, hĭj suwn :put ðəm daun ə-gen, ən wĭj -went ən :stud sam -wei ɔf. ʃuər ĭnaf -ðei suwn :ʃoud evrĭ sain əv laif ', ən bĭ:gæn tə :meik -ðɛər ĭskeip. wĭj put ðəm bæk intə ðə nest, ən kærĭd ðəm ɔf ĭn traiəmf ', fə boiz ə reklĭs ĭn -ðɛə pə:sjuwt əv pleʒə; ən wĭj :went frəm bruk tə bruk ən frəm kops tə kops, stil :faindĭŋ njuw treʒəz fər əuər ĭnseiʃəbl hændz. wĭj :faund laaks :egz, wudpidʒənz :egz ən ə handrəd ·aðə kəindz əv :egz; ən ðə big blækbəədz :nest wəz suwn fild ', ən a þraʃĭz :nest bĭsaidz.

ĭn :fækt wĭj wə sou səksesfl ðət wĭj gŏt ə lĭtl taiəd əv ĭt ', ən bĭ:gæn tə :luk əbaut əs :mɔə. ĭt wəz ə bjuwtĭfl ən solĭtrĭ kantrĭ. wĭj :stud ŏn ə hait. ðə wəz not ə ·haus tə bĭ sijn ', ĭk:sept ə solĭtrĭ faamhaus hiər ən ðɛər ĭn ðə vælĭz raund əs. ŏn ðis hait ðə wə greit wudz əv hjuwdʒ trijz wĭð ə þik andəgrouþ əv holĭ, juw, boks, ən aðər evəgrijnz.

:ðen wĭj :keim tŭ ə waid geitwei ðət :sijmd tə lijd tə -sam einʃənt mænʃən ĭn ðə wudz. ðə wə mæsĭv piləz ŏn ijtʃ said ə ðə geit; ənd ŏn ðə top əv ijtʃ pilə ðə wəz ə stoun drægən ' —ðə krest ə ðə fæmĭlĭ ðĭ ĭ:steit bĭloŋd tŭ. wĭj :lukt ət ðĭjz :drægənz wĭð wandə; ðei :fild əuə maindz wĭð ɔfl əidiəz əv ən ĭntʃaantĭd dŏmein.

bət ned :druw əs əwei -tɔdz ðĭ obdʒĭkt əv əuər ekspĭ·diʃən.

wĭj nau :sɔ ə long stijp vælĭ bĭnijþ əs', wĭð ə smɔl bruk :ranĭŋ þruw ĭt. :ðis :bruk ræn intŭ ə siərĭz əv ·fiʃpondz', whĭtʃ :lukt -verĭ ould', fə -ðɛə saidz wə ʃægĭ wĭð rijdz', ən ðə wə :þikĭts əv einʃənt þɔntrijz :skætəd əloŋ ðəm', ən ðə wə laadʒ trijz :grouĭŋ klous tə ðəm wĭð fes:tuwnz ə ðə mŏust lag-·ʒuəriənt aivĭ. ðə houl vælĭ -hæd ən :ɛər əv lounlĭnĭs ən piktʃə·resk ragĭdnĭs ðət :meid ĭt :sijm wel fitĭd fə ðĭ ə:boud əv ·fɔnz ən ·seitəz ən ðə greit god ·pæn. əz wĭj wɔkt əloŋ bəi ðə :said ə ðĭjz pondz, ən lukt daun ŏn ðə dijp, daak wɔtə, wĭj kud nt :help ə :fijlĭŋ əv ɔ: wĭj staatĭd :evrĭ təim ə fiʃ lijpt', ən lisnd soləmlĭ tə nedz tɔk əv ·otəz ðət ləəkt ĭn ðə þik mæs əv flægz n rijdz.

bət bĭhould, ·ðɛə wəz ðĭ ould tʃæpl, dijp daun ĭn ðə vælĭz. ĭt wəz ə ruwĭn', wĭð wan grei tauə :raizĭŋ hai ə-bav ðə big, grei, twistĭd trijz ðət wə :skætəd raund ĭt: ðə wər einʃənt-lukĭŋ þɔnz, lou:spredĭŋ, mosĭ meiplz, juwz, ən kræbtrijz :kavəd wĭð ĭnɔməs banʃĭz əv jelŏu misltŏu. laadʒ stounz ən hjuwdʒ :mæsĭz əv meisnrĭ :lei əbaut', :ʃouĭŋ :whot əd bĭjn ðĭ əridʒĭnəl ĭkstent ə ðə bildĭŋ. ə :flok əv dʒækdɔz ən staalĭŋz fluw:raund ðə tauə', ən :fluw in ən aut :vɛərĭəs houlz ən windŏuz :haŋ wĭð braiə', tʃætərĭŋ :ɔl ðə :taim; -ðei :sijmd tə -meik ðə solĭ-tjuwd -mɔə sensəblĭ felt.

ned maatʃt on ijgəlĭ. wij folŏud ĭn sailəns', tĭl ə radĭ wijzl ræn ə-krɔs əuə paaþ, ənd ə wudpidʒən daatĭd əut əv ə þɔn :kavəd wĭð aĭvĭ', ənd əuə boiĭʃ ijgənĭs əv kjuərĭ·osĭtĭ wəz rauzd ə-gen. wĭj ræn on, ən wə :suwn ĭn ðə :midst ə ðə mŏust intrəstĭŋ dĭskavərĭz. wĭj :faund ɔl ·kaindz əv egz: mislþraʃĭz :egz, wudpidʒənz, redstaats, red linĭts, ən :menĭ aðə kəindz əz wel.

bət ðə ruwĭnd tʃæpl wəz ðə mein :obdʒĭkt əv intərest. not ŏn ə:kaunt əv ĭts æn·tikwĭtĭ ŏr ĭts aakĭtektʃə ŏ ðə memərĭ əv ðouz berĭd andə·nijþ ĭt, bət bĭ:koz ə ðĭ ·aulz' ən aðə :streinʒ krijtʃəz wĭj ĭks:pektĭd tə faind ĭn ðĭ ould tauə. wĭj :sɔ ðə davz ən staalĭŋz :gouĭŋ in ən aut ðə tauə ˋ, ən ðə blæk swifts skrijmĭŋ raund ĭt ; ən wĭj lɔŋd, ən jet -felt :haaf əfreid tə pijp intə ðæt daak apə stɔrĭ ə ðə tauə. bət hau tə get -ðɛ̣ə ˋ? ĭt wəz ə kənsidrəbl hait ; ðə wɔlz wə dĭkeid ən broukn ˋ, ən did nt :sijm tə :giv -enĭ futhould. ned həu:evə, wĭð ɔl ðĭ ədʒilĭtĭ əv ə skuwlboi, þruw -ɔf ĭz kout, ən :dæʃĭŋ in ə-maŋ ðə grijn wildənĭs əv mælŏuz ən netlz ət ðə :fut ə ðə tauə, bĭ:gæn tŭ ĭnsəət ĭz fiŋgəz ən touz intə ðə dʒoints ə ðə meisnrĭ ; ən :ðen bĭ-gæn tə klaim ap, :verĭ -matʃ əz ə ·flai klaimz -ap ə :pein əv glaas. wĭj ·ʃadəd əz wĭj :stud bĭlou ˋ, ən :sɔ ĭm hæŋĭŋ -sam fɔtĭ fijt əbav əuə hedz ˋ, :whɛə ðə :sijmd naþĭŋ tə səpɔt ĭm ˋ, ən whŏt ·did sə:pɔt ĭm wəz kəntinjŭəlĭ kramblĭŋ andər im ˋ, ən :fel pætərĭŋ ət əuə :fijt. bət ĭn ə fjuw sekəndz ĭj wəz ət ðə :litl goþĭk belfrĭwindŏu ˋ, ən wĭð ə ʃaut əv traiəmf krept in ən disə·piəd. ə moumĭnt aaftə hĭj put əut ĭz hed, ɔl kavəd wĭð kobwebz, ən ʃautĭd '·ap wĭð jŭ ˋ, boiz ˋ, :if jŭ wont ə :sij ə sait wəəþ sijĭŋ !'

:ðis wəz sou ĭk·saitĭŋ ðət əi fəgot məi fɔmə terə, ən ræn tə ðə wɔl ən bĭ-gæn tə klaim ap ĭn ðə :seim :wei əz ·hij əd -dan ; puə web wəz əfreid. :when əi got ĭntə ðə daak pleis, əi wəz stjuwpĭfəid wĭð əstonĭʃmənt. əi d həəd əv keivz n hɔlz laitĭd wĭð ·kaabaŋklz, ən riəlĭ ĭt sijmd əz ĭf ðis pleis wə laitĭd ĭn ðə seim wei ˋ, fər əi :sɔ raund, jelŏu bɔlz əv faiə ŏn ɔl saidz ˋ, glouĭŋ mŏust ɔfl-ĭ. -ðei wə ðĭ aiz əv ·aulz ; ən ðə wəz :satʃ ə hisĭŋ ən ĭk·saitmənt, ən sətʃ ən æŋgrĭ snæpĭŋ əv bijks əz wəz wandəfl.

'·hiə -ðei aa ˋ, ·hiə -ðei aa !' :kraid ned ĭg·zaltĭŋlĭ ˋ, əz ĭj :brɔt tuw :jaŋ aulz tə ðə lait. -ðei wə ful fledʒd. 'wĭl jŭ :hæv -enĭ mɔr ?' ĭj aast ˊ. bət dʒest əz ĭj spouk, ðĭ ould :aulz ə:bav əuə :hedz :sijmd tə -get mæd wĭð reidʒ ˋ, ən dæʃt ən daatĭd əbaut ĭn ə mŏust əlaamĭŋ :wei ; ən wan ə ðəm fluw ət

:nedz feis wĭð -satʃ ə sævĭdʒ snæp ðət əi ĭks:pektĭd tə :sij ĭz ·nouz -kam ɔf. hĭj kraid aut, ən :put ĭz hænd tə ðə :pleis, ənd ĭmijdʒətlĭ əi :sɔ ðə blad strijmĭŋ dəun ĭz tʃijk. hĭj þruw ðə :jaŋ :aulz :aut ə ðəwindŏu, puld -ɔf ĭz hæt, ən stud ət bei ˎ, :redĭ tə nok :daun hĭz enĭmĭz ˎ, wĭð ə :luk əv desprĭt reidʒ. fə mai -paat, əi :þɔt ĭt moust ədvaizəbl tə bĭ ɔf; sŏu əi got əut ə ðə windŏu, ən klaimd daun wĭð ə :gudĭjl əv difĭkltĭ ən deinʒə. əi :faund hærĭ web bĭ:lou ĭn ekstəsĭz ŏuvə ðə jaŋ aulz. hĭj d kavəd ðəm ouvə wĭð ĭz hæt; ən when:evər ĭt wəz :liftĭd ap, -ðei hist əⁿ snæpt mŏust plakĭlĭ. nˈed suwn folŏud wið ĭz feis :ɔl kavəd wĭð blad ˎ, ən wĭj :faund ðĭ ould aul əd :riəlĭ teikn ə :pijs :aut əv ĭz tʃijk. wĭj stopt ðə blijdĭŋ wĭð səm fəə ˎ, ə:kɔdĭŋ tə ðə :moust əpruwvd meþəd əv skuwlboi səədʒərĭ; ən :ðen bĭ-gæn tə rĭtəən houm ˎ, wĭð əuə hændz ful əv buwtĭ. ned -hæd ðĭ aulz, web -hæd tuw nests :ful əv egz, ənd ai -hæd ðə blækbəədz :nest wĭ ðə :jaŋ pijwits ĭn ĭt.

wĭj :went ə gud -wei ap ðə vælĭ ˎ, ful əv əuə kæptʃəz ən ədventʃəz ˎ, ən tɔkĭŋ laudlĭ əbəut ðəm, -when nedz dog staatĭd ə ·kɔnkreik ĭn ə heifijld. hĭj :sed ĭz :dog kəd :ran ĭt daun; ən ðə tem·teiʃən wəz tuw stroŋ tə bĭ rĭzistĭd. sŏu ɔl:ðou wĭj wə verĭ haŋgrĭ ən raaðə taiəd ˊ, wĭj :ræn rait ĭntə ðə :midl ə ðə hai graas ˎ, wĭðaut :stopĭŋ tə rĭflekt ðət wĭj wə :duwĭŋ nŏu end əv mistʃif. wĭj wə suwn ĭn ful pəsjuwt: wan :minĭt wĭj :həəd ðə :bəəd :kraiĭŋ kreik kreik klous tuw əs, :ðen wĭj :sɔ ĭt raiz ĭn :frant ə ðə :dog, flai ə lĭtl :wei, ən :ðen :drop daun ə-gen. ĭn ðə :midl ə ðis ned hæpnd tə :luk raund; hĭj sadnlĭ -təənd peil, ən wĭð ĭz juwʒŭəl eksklə·meiʃən ‘bai dʒouv!’ :tuk tŭ ĭz hijlz ət ə trĭmendəs peis. wij lukt :raund tuw ˎ, ən :sɔ ə big kantrĭ :felŏu kamĭŋ :daun ðə hil ĭn ful tʃeis əv əs wĭðaut -meikĭŋ ə saund. ət ðis sait web ·skrijmd wĭð terə ˎ, þruw :daun ĭz nests əv egz, ən ræn fər ĭz laif. ·ai ræn tuw, jŭw mei bĭ :ʃuə; ən ðə moumĭnt ðə klodhopə njuw wĭj sɔ ĭm, hĭj :sent aaftər əs sətʃ ə terəbl həluw ðət wĭj dʒampt əz :if wĭj d bĭjn ʃot ', ən ræn on wĭð :ɔl ðə spijd ðət wəz :in əs.

ned wəz ɔl·redĭ ət ðĭ end ə ðə fijld ', ən wĭð wan lijp kræʃt þrŭw ðə hedʒ. web meid fə ðə :hedʒ ə :litl :louə daun ', ənd ·an·fɔtʃənətlĭ planʒd ĭntŭ ə bog ', whĭtʃ ĭj did nt noutĭs bĭ:koz ĭt wəz :kavəd wĭð tɔl grijn graas. hĭj sæŋk :ap tŭ ĭz weist ', ən :atəd ə mŏus pitĭfl krai əv terə ən dĭspɛə. əi :felt sou sorĭ fŏr ĭm ðət ɔl:ðou ðə terəbl mæn wəz bĭhaind mĭ, əi kud nt :help stopĭŋ ə :minĭt ən ʃautĭŋ tŭ ĭm 'fə jŏ ·laif, :hærĭ ', dæʃ on ', dæʃ on !' hĭj :meid ə desprĭt efət; ðə bog woz nt ə -verĭ waid -wan, ən ĭj :got aut əv ĭt, ən skræmbld þrŭw ðə hedʒ ɔlmŏust ət ðə seim moumĭnt. wĭj fluw əlŏŋ ðə nekst fijld wĭð breþlĭs spijd ', ən wheðə ðə :mæn :lɔst sait əv əs ŏ :not, əi kaant tel ', bət wĭj suwn :faund əuə-selvz :aut əv sait əv ĭm; ən wĭj did nt sij ĭm ə-gen tĭl wĭj :got tə ðə :top əv ə hil ', :whɛə wĭj :faund ned pæntĭŋ ən beiðd ĭn pəəspə·reiʃən ', ən steiʃənd bĭ:haind ə tɔl fəəzbaʃ ', wotʃĭŋ ðĭ enĭmĭ ', hŭw :sijmd tə bĭ kanĭŋlĭ :meikĭŋ ə səəkĭt, sŏu əz tə :teik əs bəi səpraiz. :when wĭj d :got sŏu faa ðət wĭj didnt :þiŋk ĭj d pəsjuw əs -enĭ mɔə, wĭj lei dəun ŏn ðə graas, ən traid tə -get əuə breþ ə-gen. wĭj ðen faund ðət ned ĭn ĭz flait əd :kept fəəm hould ə ðə jaŋ aulz ',—sou fəəm ĭn :fækt ðət ĭj d stræŋgld ðəm, ən stil held ðəm ĭn ĭz hændz wĭðaut nouĭŋ -ðei wə ded. əi lukt ət ðə nest əi d bĭjn kærĭĭŋ; ĭt wəz stil ðɛə, bət ðə pijwĭts əd bĭjn ʃeikn aut ən lɔst; ən :when əi þɔt əv whot məs bĭj -ðɛə feit, əi dount rĭmembər evə -hævĭŋ ə kijnə :sens əv rĭmɔs, ĭksept wans ', -when əi d :put ə houl kampənĭ əv fijldmais intŭ ə drɔə, ən fəgot ðəm. :when əi æksĭ·dentl-ĭ oupnd ðə :drɔə ə fɔtnəit aaftəwədz, əi :faund ðə puə krijtʃəz əd bĭjn :drivn bəi haŋgə tə kil ən ijt wanə:naðə; ən ðɛə sæt wan solĭtrĭ maus ĭn ðə :midst ə ðə bounz əv ĭz kəm·pænjənz, hĭmself in ðə laas steidʒ əv ĭg·zɔstʃən!

wĭj wə greitlĭ dĭsaatnd bəi əuə mĭsfətʃənz; ən wĭj wə ten təimz moə kaas daun -when wĭj þɔt ə ðə jaŋ pijwĭts; ən nau ðət wĭj wə taiəd aut, ən əd wəəkt :ɔf əuər ĭn·þjuwzĭæzm, əuə konʃənsĭz əgen :spouk aut \, ən wĭj went əlong sædlĭ ən sailəntlĭ.

wĭj wə nau bəi ðə :said ə ðə big wud wĭj d :sijn ĭn ðə mɔnĭŋ; ən ĭt :lukt əz :if wĭj wər in fər ə ·freʃ mĭs:fɔtʃən \, fə ðə dog bĭ:gæn tə -get :verĭ trablsəm: hĭj -went hantĭŋ ɔl ŏuvə ðə wud \, ən wud nt əbei nedz kɔlz. wĭj suwn :həəd ðə þandər əv ə feznts raiz klous tuw əs \, ən :ðen ðĭ ijgə baakĭŋ ə ðə dog. ned got ŏuvə ðə peilĭŋ ən :kraid ':luk hiə \, :luk hiə!' wij :klaimd ŏuvə tuw \, ən bĭhould, ðɛə wəz ə feznts :nest, ənd ət :lijst haafədazn egz ĭn ĭt! '·hiəz ə praiz \,' -sed ned \, 'wĭj l teik əm \, ən put əm -andər ə hen.' 'bət wount ĭt bĭ ·poutʃĭŋ?' -sed ai ʼ. '^ou :jes,' -sed ĭj brisklĭ \, putĭŋ ðəm ĭn ðə kraun əv ĭz hæt \, 'jŭw mə poutʃ -sam ə ðəm :if ju laik ʼ; nŏu daut -ðei l bĭ verĭ gud.' ən :ðen ĭj laaft ət ĭz oun wit. ĭn ðə :midst əv ĭz :laaftə wĭj :həəd ə braanʃ :kræk bĭhaind əs \, ən lukĭŋ raund, wĭj :sɔ ə tɔl dʒentlmən :stændĭŋ lukĭŋ -æt əs ĭntentlĭ ən sailəntlĭ. sŏu ɔf wĭj went ə:gen þrŭw ðə wud \, whəil wĭj :həəd ðə dʒentlmən :ʃautĭŋ '·stop -ðɛə \, ·stop!' bət huw d stop whəil ĭj kəd ran? \ wĭj :suwn bəəst intŭ ə :sɔt əv oupn pædək \, ən fluw ə:krɔs ĭt, wiðaut :nouĭŋ whɛər ĭt :led tŭ. evrĭ :nau ən ðen wĭj :həəd ðə dʒentlmənz dogwhisl \, ən ðə :saund :fild əs wĭð terə, ən :meid əs rĭdabl əuə spijd. tanstl ən web klaimd ŏuvər ə geit ət ðĭ aðər :end ə ðə pædək; ai dæʃt þrŭw ə gæp ĭn ðə hedʒ \, ən faund məi-self ĭn ə gaadn wĭð ə kotĭdʒ ĭn ĭt. tə məi infĭnĭt terə ai :olsŏu :sɔ ə staut -litl mæn ĭn ðə gaadn \, hŭw əz :suwn əz ĭj sɔ mĭj, ʃautĭd aut '·stop \, ai nou jŭ \, ai nou jŭ!' hĭj mait əz :wel əv :tould ðə ·san tə :stop. əi wəz ĭn ə frenzĭ əv despə·reiʃən; :whot wĭ ðə fiər əv bĭjĭŋ kɔt, ðə dĭzgreis əv bĭjĭŋ brɔt bĭ-fɔr ə mædʒĭstrĭt, ən ðə :fiər əv -sam dĭgreidĭŋ panĭʃmənt, əi wəz ləik ə mæd-mən. əi fluw þrŭw ðə gaadn :haaf blaind wĭð terə, dæʃt þrŭw ə bed ðət əd dʒes bĭjn soun ʹ—:probəblĭ wĭð anjənsijd, fər ĭt wəz plaantĭd wĭð weivĭŋ ·pijkok :feðəz tə fraitn ə-wei ðə bəədz ʹ—ən :ðen əi fel ĭntŭ ə ·kjuwkəmbəfreim wĭð ə greit kræʃ əv glaas. əi wəz nau dʒest ət ðə dɔr ə ðə kotĭdʒ, -when əi :sɔ ə :litl geit ˋ, ən dæʃt þruw ĭt ˋ, ən ət ðə seim moumĭnt əi -kɔt sait ə məi tuw felŏu fjuwdʒĭtĭvz ˋ, hŭw wə ·dʒest :ranĭŋ :intŭ ə kops. əi ræn aaftə ðəm, ən suwn ouvə·tuk ðəm. wĭj ræn əlŏŋ ə paaþ fər ə:baut haaf ə mail ˋ, ən :faindĭŋ ðə wəz nouwan aaftər əs, wĭj þruw əuə-selvz ŏn ðə graund ˋ, ouvə:kam wĭð ĭgzɔstʃən, terə, ən dĭspɛə. wĭj :lei -ðɛər ə loŋ taim ĭn sailəns ˋ, ĭk:sept ðət web ground -evrĭ :nau ən ðen; tanstl :lei wĭð ĭz feis ŏn ðə graund ĭn ə :sɔt əv salĭn æpəþi. ĭt wəz :getĭŋ daak ˋ, ən web bĭ-gæn tə :krai ‘ou diə ˋ, hau ʃl wĭj :faind əuə :wei houm ?ˋ’ əz ĭj :sed :ðis, ned dʒampt ap, ən bĭ-gæn tə :luk əbaut ĭm ˋ, əz :if tə rekə·noitə əuə pəziʃən. əz ĭj :muwvd ə :litl -wei from əs, ĭz fut strak ə-genst :samþĭŋ, ən lukĭŋ daun ĭj :sed ‘whot s ðis ˋ?’ wĭj dʒampt ap ən lukt ət ðə :pleis ˋ, ən :sɔ ə hukd steik drivn ĭntə ðə graund ˋ, ən ə stroŋ aiən tʃein faasnd tŭ ĭt. ‘:whot ĭn ðə neim əv wandə z ðis ˋ? -sed ned ˋ, ən bĭ-gæn tə þrou :ɔf ðə mos ən lijvz ðət kavəd ðə tʃein ˋ, tə sij whŏt ĭt wəz fɔə. wij :stud klous bai, wotʃĭŋ æŋʃəslĭ ˋ—·when ʃl əi fəget ðə ·horə əv -ðæt moumĭnt !—ðə wəz ə mouʃən ən ə ʃadə :andər əuə fijt, əz :if wĭj d trodn ŏn -sam livĭŋ þiŋ, ə klæŋ əv aiən, ən ə ʃrijk frəm web, ən wĭj :sɔ ĭm stændĭŋ ĭn ðə fæŋz əv ə monstrəs stijl træp !

wĭj :stud ruwtĭd ṭə ðə graund wĭð horə; bət :when wĭj :həəd ðə grounz əv puə web, ən :sɔ (h)əu dedlĭ peil ĭj :woz, wĭj lukt raund tə sij whot wĭj kəd duw. wĭj lukt ət ðə terəbl məʃijn, tə sij ĭf ĭts ɔfl aiən tijþ, whĭtʃ wĭj d sŏu ɔfn həəd ə:baut, əd piəst þrŭw ĭz þaiz ˋ, ən faund tŭ əuə greit rĭlijf ðət ĭt ·hæd nt -enĭ :tijþ; ĭt wəz sou kənstraktĭd əz tə hould ðə limz wĭðaut vaitl-ĭ indʒərĭŋ ðəm ˋ, ən :jet wĭð ə dredfl preʃər ən ægənĭ.

fə mai -paat, əi puld -æt ĭt mædlĭ ˋ, əz :if məi ĭmpeiʃənt efəts wər evə :laiklĭ tə muwv ĭt ; bət tanstl, hŭw wəz kuwlə, :ʃoud betə dʒadʒmənt: hĭj renʃt ðə hukt steik frəm ðə graund, ən puʃt ĭt ĭntə ðə mauþ ə ðə træp ˋ, ən :traid tə lijvər ĭt oupn. bət ĭt wəz ɔl ĭn vein ; ən ĭn ðə :midl əv ĭt ɔl, ə tɔl kijpə sadnlĭ əpiəd ˋ, ən :sijzd hould əv əs wĭð ə laud gəfɔ ˋ, ən :geiv ned ən mij tŭ ə mæn bĭhaind ĭm : ən :ðen :teikĭŋ ə -pijs əv aiən :aut əv ĭz pokĭt, hĭj əplaid ĭt tə ðə træp ˋ, ən wĭj :sɔ ĭt grædʒŭəlĭ oupn ĭts trĭmendəs dʒɔz. ðə mæn sijzd web wĭðaut :seiĭŋ ə wəəd ˋ, ən puld ĭm aaftər ĭm þrŭw ðə wudz ; ən ðĭ aðə :mæn dĭd ðə seim wĭð ned ən mij. wĭj suwn :faund əuə-selvz ət ə kotĭdʒ. :aaftə ðə kijpəz waif əd lukt -æt əs ən :sed -samþĭŋ əbəut ðə fiəfl wikĭdnĭs ə ðə preznt eidʒ, wĭj wə put ĭntŭ ə :sɔt əv lambərum wĭð ə mætrĭs ŏn ðə :flɔə. tə duw ðə :mæn dʒastĭs, ĭj :brɔt əs ijtʃ ə þik :hanʃ əv bred ən ə beisn əv mjlk, ən left əs -ðɛə fə ðə nait.

jŭw mĭ ĭmædʒĭn əuə fijlĭŋz. tanstl wəz salĭn ən sailənt ˋ, ən suwn -went tə slijp ; bət puə web :lei ən sobd bitəlĭ ˋ, ən preid god fəəvəntlĭ tə fəgiv ĭm ˋ, ən rĭstɔr ĭm tŭ ĭz pɛərənts ; sŏu ðət ĭn spait əv məi oun mizərĭ əi kud nt :help :putĭŋ məi aamz rəund iz nek, ən traiĭŋ tə kamfət ĭm. ou -ðæt loŋ, driərĭ nait! :wheðə wĭj slept ŏ nŏt, əi kaant tel ; bət ĭt sijmd əz ĭf ĭt əd ·nevə -kam tŭ ən end. wĭj :həəd ðĭ ould klok ĭn ðə haus :gou klik klæk ; ən evrĭ təim ĭt :strak ðĭ auə, ĭt :meid ə whizĭŋ, rɔrĭŋ saund ˋ, əz :if ĭt -æd ðĭ æsmə ; wĭj :həəd ðə krikĭts tʃəəpĭŋ noizĭlĭ ˋ, ən ·heitĭd ðə :saund ; wĭj :həəd ðə ʃaap baak ə ðə foks əutsaid ; ən evrĭ təim ðə foks baakt, ðə wotʃdog ət ðə dɔə :geiv ə dijp haul bəi -wei əv aansə ; ənd ə kok ĭn ðə lɔft ŏuvər əuə :hedz went ŏn krouĭŋ əz :if ĭj d nevə stop ; ənd ĭt :sijmd əz ĭf ðə mənĭŋ əd nevə kam. bət ĭt keim ət laast; ən :aaftə wĭj d ijtʃ -hæd ənaðə :pijs əv bred ən ə beisn əv mjlk, ðə kijpə :brɔt əs aut, ən tuk əs þrŭw ðə wudz tə ðə greit hɔl. ou ðə dizməl siŋkĭŋ ən bijtĭŋ əv əuə haats! wĭj wə gŏuĭŋ tŭ əpiə bĭ:fɔ ðə mædʒĭstrĭt əz poutʃəz ən vægəbəndz; wĭj ʃəd bĭ panĭʃt—sentənst tə pijnl səəvĭtjŭwd—præps hæŋd! ĭts nou jŭws :traiĭŋ tə dĭskraib əuə sen·seiʃənz. wĭj wə :fəəst :teikn ĭntŭ ə lobĭ ‵, -whεər ə :lot əv smaat futmən -keim ən stεəd æt əs ‵, ən dʒiəd æt əs‵, ən :meid ɔl kəindz əv flipənt ənd ĭnsaltĭŋ rĭmaaks. :ðen wĭj wə :brɔt ĭntə ðə :prezns ə ðə mædʒĭstrĭt ĭmself; ən bĭhould! ĭt wəz ðə verĭ dʒentlmən wĭj d :sijn ĭn ðə wudz. hĭz klaak ′—ə fæt -litl :mæn ĭn spektĭklz ′—wəz sitĭŋ ət ə teibl wĭð ĭz peipəz bĭfɔr ĭm; ən ðə mædʒĭstrĭt sed tŭ ĭm ‘jes′, ðijz boiz ə ðə verĭ wanz əi :sɔ jestədĭ ĭn ðĭ :ækt əv robĭŋ ə feznts :nest; ənd ĭt s wan ə ðəm ðət s :dan sŏu :matʃ mistʃĭf ĭn pætrĭk ræmzĭz gaadn. whot s ðə penltĭ fə -ðεər əfensĭz ‵?’ ‘ðə penltĭ, -səə,’ aansəd ðə klaak, lukĭŋ -æt əs þrŭw ĭz big, stεərĭŋ spektĭklz, ‘ĭz faiv paundz ijtʃ ən ðĭ ĭkspensĭz əv worənt fə ðə poutʃĭŋ, ən tə :meik ful kompĭn·seiʃən fə ðə dæmĭdʒ -dan ĭn ræmzĭz gaadn; ĭn feiljər əv ·aiðər ə ðijz pətikjələz, kə:mitmənt tə ðə :haus əv kərekʃən fə þrij manþs; ən ðæt s nŏu daut whot -ðei l get -səə; fər :if əi kən dʒadʒ bəi -ðεər əpiərəns, nou kæʃ l bĭ fɔþ kamĭŋ.’

ən truwlĭ mĭstə læŋ məit wel -teik ĭt fə graantĭd; fə tɔn əz wĭj -wəə wĭð braiəz, kavəd wĭð mad ən dast ən blad, tanstl wĭð ĭz tʃijk pætʃt wĭð fəə, ənd ɔl əv əs hægəd wĭð fətijg ən fiə, wĭj səətnlĭ :kat ə mŏus dĭsrepjətəbl figə.

:when wĭj :həəd ðĭs sentəns, wĭj lɔst ɔl kəmaand əv əuə-selvz. wĭj kraid, ĭmplɔd, ənd :ijvn daanst əbəut ðə :flɔr ĭn əuər ægənĭ əv maind. bət ĭt wəz nou juws. ðə mædʒĭstrĭt lukt ət əs sĭviəlĭ, ən tould əs to bĭ sailənt in ə laud, haaʃ vois.

ən wĭj ·wəə sailənt; ɔl ĭk-sept puə web \, hŭw nelt ət ðə fijt ə ðis ɔfl mæn \, ən raŋ ĭz hændz wĭð ə mŏust pitĭəs luk ŏn ĭz feis \, ən :kraid 'ou :səə \, diə :səə \, duw, ·duw fəgiv əs ðis wans; ĭt s məi ·bəəþdei ŏn sandĭ, ən :if jŭw l ounlĭ fəgiv əs, əi l send jŭ -sam əv məi plam pudĭŋ.' ðə naa·ijvtĭ əv ðĭs ə:dres wəz tuw matʃ fə ðə wəəðĭ mæn: fər ə :moumĭnt ĭj stɛəd ət ðə :boi ĭn sailənt əstonĭʃmənt \, ən :ðen ĭj :put ĭz hændz tŭ ĭz saidz, ən bəəst ĭntŭ ə laud :fit əv laaftə. ĭt wəz sam taim bi:fɔr ĭj kəd kəmpouz ĭm-self; ənd ĭz fæt -litl klaak ekŏud ĭz maastəz brɔd laaf wĭð ə tʃaklĭŋ hee, hee, hee, ən ðə rĭmaak 'wel \, ĭf ðæt ĭznt klevə!'

ət leŋþ ðə mædʒĭstrĭt put on ə siərĭəs kauntĭnəns \, :ðou ĭt wəz evĭdənt ĭj kəd haadlĭ :kijp ĭm-self frəm bəəstĭŋ əut ·laafĭŋ ə:gen. :ðen ĭj :sed 'jŏ bəəþdei /, məi boi /—ən huw ə juw \?' ':ou əi m hærĭ web, hærĭ web -səə.' '·web/,' -sed ðə mædʒĭstrĭt, 'whŏt ʃuəlĭ jŏ :not ðə san əv mĭstə web əv heizfəd?' 'ou ·jes əi æm sə; whot l məi puə pəpaa ən məmaa :duw! ou whot ·wil -ðei duw!' ðə mædʒĭstrĭt :sijmd səpraizd \, ən :sed 'ən huw ə ðĭ ·aðə :tuw \?' hærĭ neimd mij; ən ðə mædʒĭstrĭt :sed 'gud hevnz! hau dĭd jŭ :get ĭntə ðis kən:diʃən \? ən hau dĭd jŭ :kam tə bĭ teikĭŋ məi feznts :nest? huw z ðĭs aðə :boi?' 'ou -səə, ĭt s ned tanstl.' 'ned tanstl!' ĭks:kleimd ðe mædʒĭstrĭt; ^aa, əi sij ĭt :ɔl :nau. tanstl \, əi v ·həəd əv jŏ duwĭŋz. əi v həəd əv ə səətn grei ·teriə jŭ :kijp tə dĭstəəb :ɔl ðə geim ĭn ðə pærĭʃ. ^aiv həəd əv jŭ, ^ai kən tel jŭ. sŏu jŭ :kijp ə ^ferĭt—ənd ə net tŭw \—tə kætʃ ræbĭts. ən jŭw nou həu tə get ə-krɔs ðə pond ĭn ə woʃtab \, ən -get :on tə ðə herənailənd \, ən klaim ðə big trijz ĭn ðə herənrĭ ĭn :spait əv tentəhuks n :ɔl. əi l tel jŭ ·whot \, -maastə tanstl \, jŭw l -get ·hæŋd :wan ə ðĭjz deiz.'

ðə mædʒĭstrĭt :ðen :ræŋ ə bel \, ən ə mæn :keim in. hĭj pointĭd ət web ən mij, ən :sed 'hiə \, teik ðĭjz tuw boiz tə

-ðɛə pɛərənts: nŏu daut -ðɛər æŋʃəs əbəut ðəm; ən juw, mĭstə læŋ, :send ə nout wĭð ijtʃ ə ðəm tŭ ĭksplein -andə whot səəkəmstənsĭz -ðei keim bĭfɔ mĭj, ən :giv ðəm propə wɔnĭŋ əv jaŋ tanstl. əi ʃl :send ᵛðæt :boi tŭ ĭz faaðə wĭð ə nout əv ə ^difrənt :kaind.'

wĭj wə nau rĭlijst frəm ðə terəz əv ĭmpriznmənt ən pijnl səəvitjŭwd ən hæŋĭŋ; bət əi ʃl nevə fə:get əuə ʃeim ən hjŭwmilĭ·eiʃən :when wĭj :keim houm. ĭt wəz ə brait, hot samə dei; :evrĭþĭŋ əraund əs :sijmd to rĭpouz ĭn bjuwtĭ ən hæpĭnĭs; whəil wij -keim houm hægəd, tætəd, ən dĭgreidĭd \, ləik sou -menĭ prodigəl sanz. ɔl əuə glɔrĭ wəz :təənd ĭntə dĭzaastər ən kəntemt. wĭj -keim houm wĭð ə :sens əv ijvl ə:pon əs \, ənd əuə haats wə sɔə when wĭj þɔt əv ðĭ æŋ·zaĭĭtĭ ən dĭstres əv əuə pɛərənts.

əi wount :trai tə dĭskraib əuə rĭsepʃən -when wĭj -keim houm \—ðə dʒoifl səpraiz \, ðə wɔm ĭmbreis \, ðə tiəz \, ən ðĭ ekspl ə·neiʃənz ðæt :folŏud \, ən ðə rĭpruwfs. ĭts ĭnaf tə sei ðət ðis ekspĭ·diʃən tə ðĭ ould tʃæpl əz bĭjn ə lesn tŭ əs ɔl əuə laivz. ĭt ʃoud əs həu juwslĭs ĭt :iz tə sijk pleʒə ĭksept ĭn ðə paaþ əv onər ən streit·fɔwədnĭs.

ðə jaŋ ræt.

ðə wəz wans ə jaŋ ræt ŭw wud nt -teik ðə trabl tə :meik -ap ĭz maind. :when ðĭ aðə :ræts aast ĭm ĭf ĭj d :laik tə -kam aut wĭ ðəm ət nait, hĭj d :sei 'əi doun(t) nou \,' ən :when -ðei :sed 'wŭd jŭ :laik tə :stop ət houm?' hĭj stil sed 'əi doun nou': hĭj wud nt -teik ðə trabl tə :meik ə tʃois, ŏ setl whitʃ ĭj :laikt best.

wan dei ən ould :grei ræt sed tŭ ĭm \ ':nau luk hiə \ —nou -wan l evə kɛə fə jŭ, ĭf jŭ gou on ləik ðis. jŭw v nou -mɔə maind ðən ə :bleid əv graas! ĭt mei bĭ gud tə giv -ap jŏr oun :wei samtəimz, bət ĭt s not gud tə -hæv nou :wei əv jŏr :oun ətɔl.'

ðə jaŋ ræt sæt ap ən lukt waiz, bət sed naþĭŋ.

'dount jŭ ·þiŋk sŏu‵?' :sed ðĭ oul :grei ræt‵, ənd ĭj :geiv ə stæmp wĭð ĭz fut; fər ĭj kud nt ·bɛə tə :sij ðə jaŋ :ræt sŏu ·koulbladĭd.

'əi doun nou' wəz ɔl ðə jaŋ :ræt sed; ən :ðen ĭj wɔkt ɔf wĭð slou steps‵, tə ·þiŋk fər ən auə :wheðər ĭj ʃəd :stei ət houm ĭn ĭz houl, ŏ gou aut ĭn ðə lɔft.

wan dei ðə wəz ə greit noiz ĭn ðə lɔft. ĭt wəz ə -verĭ ould :lɔft‵, ən ðə ruwf let ĭn ðə rein‵, ən ðə bijmz wər ɔl rotn‵, sŏu ðə :pleis woz nt seif tə liv ĭn. ət laast wan ə ðə dʒoists -geiv wei‵, ən ðə bijm fel wĭð wan end ŏn ðə flɔə. ðə wɔlz ʃuk, ən ɔl ðə ræts hɛə :stud ŏn end wĭð frait.

'ðis woun(t) duw‵' -sed ðĭ ould ræts, ən -ðei ʃuk -ðɛə grei hedz əz -ðei spouk‵, 'wĭj məs lijv ðis :pleis.'

sŏu -ðei :sent əut skauts tə luk fər ə njuw houm. ĭn ðə nait ðə skauts :keim bæk, ən :sed -ðei d :faund ən ould baan‵, :whɛə ðə d bĭ rum ən fuwd fə ðəm ɔl.

'-ðen wĭj d betə -gou ət ·wans‵' -sed ðĭ ould :ræt‵, hŭw wəz tʃijf; :ðen ĭj :geiv ðĭ ɔdə 'fɔm ĭn lain!'

ðə ræts -keim aut ə -ðɛə houlz, ən :stud ŏn ðə flɔr ĭn ə loŋ lain.

'ə jŭ ɔl hiə?' -sed ðĭ ould :ræt, ən ĭj lukt raund‵—'həv jŭ ɔl dĭsaidĭd tə gou?— :meik -ap jŏ maindz ət ·wans.'

'jes‵, jes‵' :sed ɔl ðə ræts ĭn ðə lain.

dʒes ðen ðĭ ould :ræt -kɔt sait əv jaŋ grip′— :ðæt wəz ðə jaŋ :ræts neim′— : hĭj woz nt ·in ðə :lain, ənd ĭj woz nt ĭg:zæktlĭ aut·said ĭt: hĭj :stud dʒes bai ĭt.

'jŭ did nt ·spijk, :grip‵' :sed ðĭ ould ræt‵, 'əv kɔs jŏ kamĭŋ.'

'əi doun nou\' :sed grip.

'dount nou' ! :whai jŭ doun :þiŋk ĭt s ·seif :duw jŭ ?'

'əi doun nou'' :sed grip; 'ðə ruwf mei nt :kam doun jet'.'

'wel\, stei -ðen\' :sed ənaðə :ræt\, 'ən səəv jŭ rait ĭf jŏ kild.'

'əi doun nou ðət əi l stei'' :sed grip ; 'ðə ruwf ·mait :kam daun suwn'.'

'wel\' -sed ðĭ ould ræt, 'wĭj kaant weit fə jŭw tə :meik -ap jŏ maind. rait əbaut feis ! maatʃ !'

ən ðə loŋ lain ·maatʃt əut ə ðə lɔft. daun ðə :steps -ðei went, wan bəi wan\, whəil ðə jaŋ ræt :lukt on.

'əi ·þiŋk əi l :gou'' hĭj sed tŭ ĭmself, 'bət jet əi doun nou'; ĭt s :nais ən snag hiə'.'

ðə teil ə ðə laast ræt wəz lɔs tə sait əz ĭj spouk. hĭj went tə ðə steps ən lukt daun. 'əi l :gou -bæk tə məi houl fər ə :bit,' -sed :hij, 'dʒes tə :meik -ap məi maind.'

ðæt nait ðə wəz ə greit kræʃ. daun -keim bijmz, dʒoists, tailz'—ðə houl ruwf.

nekst dei səm men :keim tə :luk ət ðə lɔft. ðei :þɔt ĭt od -ðei did nt -sij :enĭ ræts ; bət ət laast wan ə ðəm :hæpnd tə muwv ə big tail, ən ĭj :sɔ ə jaŋ ræt, kwait ded, haaf in ən haaf aut əv ĭts houl.

waild laif.

1.

gŭd mɔnĭŋ ; jŏr ap əəlĭ : əi :houp jŭ slept :wel\—əi :houp ðĭ ·aulz :did nt dĭstəəb jŭ. ^ou, wəz ðæt aulz ! : əi :həəd ə mŏust an·əəþlĭ skrijtʃĭŋ\— ĭt :sijmd tə -kam frəm ə trij dʒest əut:said məi windŏu ; bət əi wəz tuw taiəd fər ĭt tə :kijp mĭj əweik ˎ— bĭsaidz ˎ, :aaftə ðə landən kæts -wan ɔt tə bĭ :eibl tə stænd ɔlmŏust ˙enĭþĭŋ ĭn ðə :wei əv nŏktəənl mjuwzĭk. -let s -teik ə :təən ĭn ðə gaadn tĭl brekfəst s :redĭ. jes ˎ, əi ʃəd laik tə -sij jŏ :gaadn : əi ounlĭ -kɔt ə glims əv ĭt laas(t) nait ; jŭw v :got səm fain trijz : whŏt ə məgnifĭsənt elm ! ; :iz nt -ðæt ðə trij -whɛə ðĭ ˙aul wŏz :laas :nait ? : -when əi :lukt aut əv windŏu, əi :þɔt əi :sɔ -samþĭŋ whait wĭð lɔŋ iəz ləik ə kæts. jes ˎ, -ðei v gŏt ə nest ĭn :ðæt :trij ; :if jŭ laik, əi l ʃou jŭ ðə jaŋ ˙aulz sam dei. jes ˎ, əi ʃəd laik tə sij ðəm : əi m verĭ -matʃ intrĭstĭd ĭn nætʃərəl histrĭ. tɔkĭŋ əv aulz, ə kjuəriəs :þiŋ :hæpnd tŭ ə boi ə:baut :hiə. hĭj :faund ən aulz :nest ĭn ə trij wĭ ðə jaŋ -wanz in ĭt. sŏu ĭj tuk ðə :jaŋ :aulz, ən klaimd daun əz faast əz ĭj kud ˎ, ən dʒest əz ĭj :got tə ðə graund, ðĭ ould :aul -keim bæk tə ðə nest ˎ, ən :when ʃĭj :faund ðə jaŋ -wanz əd bĭjn teikn, ʃĭj -meid ə swuwp ət ðə boi. ðə :boi þruw ĭm-self ŏn ĭz bæk ən stak -ap ĭz hobneild buwts ĭn ðə :wei kantrĭ :boiz :duw -when -ðei :wont tə dĭfend ðəm-selvz ˎ, ən ðĭ ould aul dæʃt ə-genst ðə aiən ə ðə buwts wĭð satʃ fɔs ðət ʃĭj fel :daun stand ˎ, ən :sou ðə :boi :got ðĭ ould :aul əz wel əz ðə jaŋ -wanz. :boiz ɔt nt tə bĭ əlaud tə teik jaŋ bəədz ; :if -ðei :teik ən eg :nau ən :ðen, ˙ðæt ɔt tə bĭ ĭnaf. jes ˎ, əi juws(t) tə :trai ən ĭmpres -ðæt ŏn -ðɛə maindz -when əi fəəst -keim hiə ; bət əi suwn :geiv ĭt ap ˎ— ĭt wəz nou juws : ðə pijpl əbaut :hiər :ounlĭ laaf ət jŭ -when jŭ :tɔk əv hjŭwmænĭtĭ : əi riəli :þiŋk -ðei doun :nou whot ðə :wəəd mijnz.

ə fain dog :ðæt ! bət raaðə sævĭdʒ : :hau ĭj ˙baakt ət mĭj laas nait ! : hĭj niəlĭ :brouk ĭz tʃein :traiĭŋ tə get ət mĭj. hĭj þɔt jŭ wər ə træmp ˎ, ŏr ə dʒəəmən bænd. jŭ doun :mijn tə :sei jŭ -get dʒəəmən bændz ĭn ðĭs autəðəwei pleis ? ^ou jes ˎ, :samtəimz tuw ŏ :þrij ə wijk ; ŏ :raaðə, wĭj ᵛjuwst tə -hæv ðəm : -ðei doun ˙kam :nau : ðə dog :kijps ðəm ə:wei ˎ—

træmps :tuw bəi ðə dazn ; tĭl ət laast taigə ·bit :wan ə ðəm ; sins ðen wĭj hæv nt -hæd ə siŋgl wan.

əi :sij jŭw v ounlĭ ·waild flauəz ĭn jŏ gaadn. jes ˎ, :ðæt s :wan ɔv məi fænsĭz : əi doun kɛə mətʃ fə ·gaadn flauəz. əi dount maind ə fjŭw ouldʄæʃənd :gaadn :flauəz ĭn frant, -satʃ əz swijt pijz, dʒĭreinjəmz, fjuwʃəz, :swijt wiljəmz ən sou ŏn, bət əi v :meid ðə bæk -ɔlmŏust ĭntaiəlĭ ĭntŭ ə waild :gaadn ˎ, ĭk:sept ðət əi -hæv ə :fjuw forĭn ʃrabz. bət sam ə :ðouz :ʃrabz jŭ :sij ðɛər ə sou nætʃərələizd ðət jŭ kən haadlĭ :kɔl ðəm forĭn : -ðei grou waild ĭn menĭ -paats əv iŋglənd. jes ˎ, əi v :sijn roudə·dendrənz :grouĭŋ waild ĭn ðə njuw forĭst. ðɛə, :luk ət -ðæt bæŋk əv ·foksglavz ˎ — whot **kən** bĭ mɔə gɔdʒəs ? -ðei l :gou ŏn flauərĭŋ ɔl þrŭw ðə samə. ĭn ðə spriŋ :ðæt :bæŋk s :kavəd wĭð primrouzĭz ˎ ən kauslĭps ˎ ən okslĭps ˎ ən ənemənĭz ˎ ən waild haiəsĭnþs. hiər əi v gŏt ə bæŋk əv flauərĭŋ graasĭz. nau əi l ʃou jŭ məi ·fəəngaadn ; əi bĭlijv əi v gŏt evrĭ :fəən ðət :grouz ĭn ðə britĭʃ ailəndz ŏn ðijz bæŋks. whot s ðæt ˎ ?: :iz ĭt ə fəən ? jes ˎ, ĭt s ðĭ ŏzmandə rĭgeilĭs. whai ˎ, -ðæt s komən ˈbrækĭn ! ; əi þɔt ĭt :wud nt grou ĭn ə gaadn. ^ou, əi v gŏt ·daznz əv plaants :hiə ðət ə səpouzd not tə :grou ĭn ə gaadn. mous :pijpl doun :nou :hau tə træns·plaant : jŭw kən træns:plaant enĭþĭŋ ˎ, əz :loŋ əz jŭ dount dĭstəəb ðə ruwts : :ðæt s ðə houl sijkrĭt. əv :kɔs, jŭ məs :get ðə rait soil ˎ, ən ðə rait ĭkspouʒə ən sou ŏn, ən ðæt s ðə :mous difĭklt :paat əv ĭt. əi :faind ðət plaants ə dʒes ləik hjuwmən bijĭŋz : jŭ wont ə :səətn tækt tə mænĭdʒ ðəm. aaftər ɔl, ðə z naþĭŋ -mɔə bjuwtĭfl ðən ðə komən meil :fəən. jes ˎ, ən ĭt s -wan ə ðə haadĭĭst : ĭt l :grou enĭwhɛə. ĭt s ə greit ədvaantĭdʒ -hævĭŋ ðĭs :litl bruk ; jŭw :sij əi v :meid ĭt ĭntŭ ə :kaind əv ·maaʃ :louə daun, :sou ðət əi kən :grou evrĭ kəind əv wɔtəplaant. :ðijz fə·getmĭnots ə verĭ fain.

-daz -ðæt ·wud bĭloŋ t jŭw? jes\: ĭt s ounlĭ ə smɔl kops. əi v gŏt ə pædək ŏn ðĭ :aðə :said fə ðə hɔsĭz. -ðæt rĭmaindz mĭ\— :who də jŭ :sei tŭ ə ·raid :aaftə brekfəst\?; əi doun þiŋk ĭt l bĭ tuw hot/. ðə z ·naþĭŋ əi ʃəd laik betə\, :if jŭ kən :let mĭ -hæv ə kwaiət hɔs: əi m :not -matʃ əv ə raidə, ənd əi m aut əv præktĭs. ɔl rait/; jŭw ʃl -hæv nɔvl: hĭj z ə stedĭ :ould hɔs\ — ə ·beibĭ kəd raid ĭm\ — worəntĭd frij frəm vais. tempər əv ə læm, ən ækʃən əv ə stijmenʒĭn\, əi sə:pouz. ĭgzæktlĭ sŏu: hĭz ·greit :merĭt iz ðət ĭj nevə ʃaiz ət enĭþĭŋ\— not :ijvn ət ə ·trækʃənenʒĭn; hĭz ounlĭ folt iz ðət ĭj z :raaðə :givn tə ·baitĭŋ; bət jŭ nijd nt bĭ əlaamd: hĭj ounlĭ :baits ĭn ðə steibl: -when ĭj z gŏt ĭz braidl ŏn ĭj z ɔl rait.

2.

wel, ə jŭ redĭ? əi doun :fijl kwait rait. ŏu, əi ^sij, jŏ ·stirəps ə tuw loŋ: ælfrĭd ʃl ʃɔtn ðəm ə :litl\ — ĭz ðæt :rait? jes\: ĭt s ɔl :rait nau. weit ə :minĭt: əi məs taitn məi gəəþs. əi :sij nɔvl z freʃə ðən əi þɔt ĭj wŏz: jŭ məst hould ĭm ·in ə :bit gouĭŋ :daun hil; ðəz ə :lot əv luws ·stounz əbəut: hĭj mait -kam daun. ʃl wĭj :get ŏn tə ðə hai ·roud :suwn? jes\, hiə wĭj aa. wel\, :whitʃ :wei ʃl wĭj gou\? ðər iz nt :matʃ tʃois/: :ðis ĭz ðĭ ounlĭ :dijsnt roud ðər iz ə:baut :hiə, ĭk:sept ðə :wan ðət gouz raund bəi ·gædbruks\ — ðis :roud :lijdz intŭ ĭt; ʃəl wĭj gou raund ðæt wei, ən bæk :ouvə hætʃbərĭ daun, sŏu əz tə -get ə vjuw ə ðə muəz? jes\, :lets :gou ðæt -wei.

·hal·lou/! mɔə sainz əv sivl-əi·zeiʃən! whot ə gɔdʒəs kəməəʃəl trævl-ə! d jŭ :mijn ðə :mæn ðət :dʒes paast əs ĭn ðə pounĭtræp? jes\, ðæt rĭsplendənt indĭ:vidʒuəl wĭð ðə whait hæt\ ən ðə velvĭt kout\ ən ðə skaalĭt tai: əi nevə :sɔ sətʃ ə bleiz əv kalə; ĭt səətnlĭ -daz nɔvl kredĭt ðət ĭj did nt

·ʃai ət ĭm. ^ðæt iz nt ə kəməəʃəl trævlə ′: ĭt s əuə ·doktə; hĭj z kwait ə dʒentlmən ‵, :ðou jŭ :wud nt þiŋk sŏu tə luk ət ĭm. iz ĭj ən em dij? ou nŏu ‵, ĭj z ounlĭ ən em sij es ′.

jɔə :hɔs :sijmz kwaiət ĭ:naf. hĭj z not sŏu kwaiət əz ĭj luks. hĭj gouz ŏn ɔl rait fə manþs təgeðə ‵, ən :ðen sadnlĭ -teiks ə :fit əv viʃəsnĭs ‵ — ʃaiz ət :ɔlmŏust evrĭþĭŋ. bət ĭj z matʃ :betə nau ðən ĭj ·juws tə bĭj. fər əbaut siks manþs ĭj :juws tə ʃai regjələlĭ ət tʃæpmənz hæt. əi dount wandə. əi did nt :maind ĭt raidĭŋ, bət ĭt wəz raaðə ɔkwəd ·draivĭŋ: hĭj :juwst tə bæk ‵, ən trai tə ran -ap ðə bæŋk; bət əi kjuəd ĭm. :hau dĭd jŭ mænĭdʒ ðæt ‵? :ou, əi :got tʃæpmənz hauskijpə tə lend mĭj -wan əv ĭz ould hæts whəil ĭj wəz əwei ‵, ən taid it tŭ ən ould fiʃĭŋrod sŏu əz tə dæŋgl bĭ:fɔr ĭz aiz —. ·huwz aiz ‵, tʃæpmənz ′? nou ‵, ðə hɔsĭz; wel ‵, əi drouv ĭm ap ən daun ĭn ðis -wei ĭn :frant ə ðə tænjaad ‵, ən :sou əi kild tuw bəədz wĭð wan stoun. bət ĭj nevə gŏt kwait juws tə ðə tænjaad tĭl əi sent ælfrĭd tə -get ə botl ə ðə wɔtə -ðei tæn wĭð ‵, ən woʃt ĭz nouz wĭð ĭt evrĭ dei fər ə wijk; aaftə ðæt ĭj did nt maind ðə :smel.

ĭz -ðæt kjuəriəs straktʃər ə ·paund? jes ‵, -ðæt s ðə vilĭdʒ paund. jŭ dount :sij menĭ ə ðəm nauədeiz. nou ‵, ən ðis -wan z -gouĭŋ tə ruwĭn ləik evrĭþĭŋ els əbaut hiə. ĭts tʃijf :juws :sijmz tə :bij tə :səəv əz ə prop fə ðə vilĭdʒ aidləz ‵— samþĭŋ tə lijn ə-genst ən gosĭp ɔl :dei loŋ. jes ‵, ĭf :wij wə tə kam bæk ðis wei wĭðin ðə nekst siks auəz, wĭj ʃəd :sij ðouz :þrij men launʒĭŋ ĭn ĭgzæktlĭ ðə seim ætitjŭwdz ‵, ən wĭj ʃəd :sij ðæt boi pəətʃt on ðə top reil wĭð ðə seim evə·laastĭŋ grin ŏn ĭz kauntĭnəns. daz nt ĭj rĭmaind jŭ əv koulrĭdʒĭz dĭskripʃən ‵

:tiz ə puər idjət boi
hŭw sits ĭn ðə san ‵, ən twəəlz ə bau əbaut ‵,
hĭz wijk aiz sijðd ĭn :moust an·mijnĭŋ tiəz.

ən :sou ĭj sits ˋ, sweiĭŋ ĭz kounləik hed ;
ən stɛərĭŋ ət ĭz bau frəm mɔn tə sanset,
·sij·sɔz ĭz vois ĭn ĭnaa·tikjŭlĭt noizĭz !

ĭk·sept ðət ðis :boi :sijmz tə -teik ə mɔə tʃiəfl :vjuw əv laif.

:ðæt s ə fain :ould haus ! jes ˋ, -ðæt s gædbruks :pleis. kædbruk ˊ ? nou ˋ, ;gædbruk ˋ— wĭð ə dʒij. :mas bĭ :raaðə ·dæmp :ðou daun ðɛə. jes ˋ, ĭt s ləik ɔl :ðijz ould hauzĭz ; ðĭ ould əidiə woz ˊ : :faind ðə dijpĭst ən dæmpĭst houl jŭ kæn, ən :bild ət ðə botəm əv ĭt ; ðə z ɔlwĭz ə puwl əv wɔtə bĭ:fɔə gædbruks hɔl dɔr ĭn ðə wintə. bət ·jɔə :haus iz nt ləik ðæt ˊ. nou ˋ, mai :haus ĭz ɔl rait ˊ ; bət ĭt s ðĭ ounlĭ drai haus ĭn ðə houl :kantrĭ raund. əi hæd ĭt :bilt on pəəpəs. ðə mæn ŭw -hæd ðĭ ould :haus bĭfɔə mĭj daid əv rŭwmætĭk fijvə ˋ, sŏu əi puld ĭt daun, ən bilt ənaðə -wan haiər ap.

·hal·lou -ðɛə z gædbruk ĭmself ! ·kjuəriəslukĭŋ mæn ; :samþĭŋ ĭn ðə glædstən :stail. jes ˋ, ən ĭj z laik glædstən ĭn meni :weiz : hĭj -æz ðə :seim ĭgzjuwbərənt vəitælĭtĭ ˋ, ən ðə :seim aiən konstĭ·tjuwʃən ˋ — :verĭ vəəsətəil :tuw ˋ — ɔltə·geðər ə verĭ rĭmaakəbl mæn. əi :dɛəsei ĭj l :kam raund ðĭs aaftə-·nuwn : əi :sɔ ĭm lukĭŋ ət jŭw ; hĭj z ɔlwĭz intrĭstĭd ĭn njuw pijpl. bət luk hiə ˋ, ĭt s -getĭŋ leit : əi m əfreid wĭj ʃl bĭ leit fə lanʃ ĭf wĭj gou bæk :ouvə ðə daunz ; præps wĭj d betə -gou bæk ðə wei wĭj keim. ɔl rait ˊ : əi m :getĭŋ :raaðə taiəd.

bai dʒouv ! ðɛər ə :ðouz þrij men ən ðæt boi stil ðɛə ! jes ˋ, ən whot s mɔə wandəfl, stil ĭn:geidʒd ĭn konvə·seiʃən. :whot ŏn ·əəþ də -ðei :faind tə tɔk əbəut ˋ? :ou, matʃ ðə :seim sabdʒĭkts əz landən :men tɔk əbəut ĭn -ðɛə klabz.

3.

:hau d jŭ fijl :aaftə jŏ ˈraid :jestədĭ ˎ?—raaðə stifˊ—? jesˎ, ən sɔə tuw: əi kən haadlĭ si daun. wel -ðenˎ, əi :þiŋk wĭj d :betə gĭv ap əuər əi:diə əv draivĭŋ tə stokbrĭdʒ; sə:pouz wĭj :gou fər ə stroul ŏuvə ðə daunzˎ? jesˎ, əi ʃəd laik ðætˎ —ðə z naþĭŋ əi ʃəd laik betə; bət əi məs rait səm ˈletəz :fəəstˎ, if jŭ dount :maind weitĭŋ haafən:auə. jŭw d betə kam ĭntə mai ˈden: wĭj ʃaant bĭ dĭstəəbd -ðɛə. bai ðə bai, :hiə z səm ˈsijlĭŋwæks: jŭw d betə sijl -ap jŏ letəz; :ai ɔlwĭz dŭw. whai d jŭ dŭw ðætˎ? welˎ, jŭ :sijˎ, ĭn ə smɔl :pleis ləik ðis ðə z ə :gudĭjl əv kjuərĭˈosĭtĭ əbəut aðə :pijplz əfɛəz; ən wĭj faind ðət :if wĭj :dount sijl əuə :letəz, -ðei -get oupnd ət ðə poustɔfĭs. əi doun ˇnou ðət -ðei evə -went sŏu faar əz tŭ oupn̩ -enĭ letəz əv ˇmain, bət sevrəl əv məi səəvənts əv kəmpleind əv ĭt: jaŋ wimĭn dount :laik -hævĭŋ -ðɛə lavəfɛəz tɔkt ŏv ɔl ŏuvə ðə vilĭdʒ. əz :suwn əz əi kən -get pozĭtĭv pruwf əv ĭt, əi ʃl rait tə ðĭ əþorĭtĭzˎ, ən get -əə :təənd əwei. həə?: ĭz ĭt ə wumən? jesˎ: ðɛə ʃij iz: ðɛə z ðə pousmistrĭs həəˈself. d jŭ :hiə ðə dog :baakĭŋ? ĭt s kjuəriəs həu ĭj heits :ðæt :wumən. nekst tə həər ĭj -æz ðə greitĭst ænˈtipəþĭ tə ˈgædbruk; əi :hæv tə :tʃein ĭm ap whenˈevə -ðei ə:piər ŏn ðə sijn. hiər ə ˈtuw :letəz fə juw, ən tuw njuwspeipəz fə mij. :if jŏ redĭ, wĭj l staat ət wansˎ, bĭ:fɔr ĭt -gets :tuw hot.

ə pritĭ kotĭdʒ -ðæt! -ðæt s sɔjəz :kotĭdʒ; ĭf jŭ laik, jŭ kən :sij ðĭ inˈsaid. nouwan ət houm ĭk:sept ðə beibĭ; ĭt s :kwait ə piktʃə :iz nt ĭtˎ—ðə kreidl bəi ðə faiə, ən ðə big ʃijpdog stretʃt aut bĭsaid ĭt. əi nevə :sɔ sətʃ ə primĭtĭv :pleis bifɔr ĭn məi laif. moust ə ðə leibərəz kotĭdʒĭz ə:baut :hiə ə :bilt ĭn ðis :stail: wan big rum wĭð ə stoun flɔr ən ə hjuwdʒ tʃimnĭ. nou haaþ, əi pə:sijv: ə faiər əv logz ŏn ðə bɛə flɔə; :who dəz -ðæt dɔə :lijd tŭ\`?; əi sə:pouz -ðæt s ðə bedrum. ou nŏu\`, -ðei slijp ĭn ðə lɔft\`, ap stɛəz: ðæt dɔə lijdz tə ðə ·dɛərĭ; sɔjə z betər ɔf ðən jŭw d þiŋk: hĭj -æz tʃaadʒ ə ðə ·faam wĭj dʒes paast. :who d jŭ kɔl -ðæt tæŋgld wildənĭs ə faam? wel\`, ĭt s gŏuĭŋ :raaðər əut əv kaltĭ·veiʃən ləik ə gud -menĭ ə ðə faamz ə:baut :hiə; -ðei ounlĭ :kijp ə :fjuw kauz -ðɛər ĭn ðə samə; :in ðə wintə -ðei briŋ :daun ɔl ðə kætl frəm ðĭ aðə :faam :haiər ap ĭn ðə vælĭ\`— ĭt s tuw kould fə ðəm -ðɛər ĭn ðə wintə. wel\`, wĭj d betə bĭ muwvĭŋ on: ĭt s haaf :paas ten\`— sɔjəz lanʃtəim. :if -ðei lanʃ ət haaf :paas ten, -ðei mast -æv brekfəst pritĭ əəlĭ. ^ou nŏu, -ðei nevə -get ap bĭ:fɔr eit. :when də -ðei dain -ðen\`? :ou, ə:baut haaf :paas twelv. who də -ðei -hæv fə dinə\`? :ou, ə hjuwdʒ mijt pai\`, ŏr ə stjuw əv tuw ŏ :þrij difrənt kəindz əv mijt. ðen -ðei -hæv tij, ən ɔfn ə ·sekənd :tij\`, ən waind ap wĭð ə hevĭ sapə. -ðen əi sə:pouz -ðei dount -get tə bed tĭl ə:baut ĭlevn ŏ twelv. ^ou nŏu, -ðɛə :dʒenrəlĭ ĭn bed bəi eit əklok; ŏn sandĭz -ðei get -ap leitə ən gou tə :bed əəlĭə. jŭ mas nt ĭ:mædʒĭn -ðɛər ·ɔl ləik ðis: ðə :pijpl ət ðə nekst :faam ə kwait difrənt: -ðei get -ap ət faiv, ən wəək haad ɔl dei; bət ·ðei kam frəm ə difrənt -paat ə ðə kantrĭ. ĭt s ə kjuərĭəs þiŋ, bət whɛər əi wəz steiĭŋ wĭð ə ·frend laast samə´ —:samwhɛər in hæmʃiə´— hĭj :sed ðə pijpl ə ðə vilĭdʒ wə sou leit əv getĭŋ ap ĭn ðə mɔnĭŋ; hĭj :sed ðət kantrĭ :pijpl wə :riəli matʃ leiziə ðən taun :pijpl\`— ət enĭ -reit ĭn ðə ·sauþ əv iŋglənd. wel\`, fə wan þĭŋ -ðei nevə wɔk, ĭf -ðei kən help ĭt\`—. :hiə z sɔjə :kamĭŋ houm tŭ ĭz lanʃ. :whɛə z ĭz waif\`? :ou, ʃĭj z ɔlwĭz gæðĭŋ əbaut ən gosĭpĭŋ wĭ ðə neibəz\`— :gɔn tŭ -əə maðəz, əi sə:pouz; əi ʃud nt wandər ĭf sɔjə :hæd tə kuk ĭz oun dinə. wel\`, əi wəz :seiĭŋ ðət kantrĭ :pijpl nevə wɔk. nəu ðis sɔjə z ə big, strɔŋlukĭŋ :felŏu´— :ðou ĭj iz nt sŏu strɔŋ əz ĭj luks´—, bət :if jŭ wə tŭ aask ĭm tə wɔk tə ðə vilĭdʒ ′— ə litl :ouvə tuw mailz ′— hĭj d þiŋk ĭt ðə greitĭst haadʃĭp jŭ kəd posəblĭ ĭnflikt ŏn ĭm; hĭj d :teik ə poul əz loŋ əz hĭmself ‵, ən stop tə si daun ən groun evrĭ ten minĭts. ənaðə þĭŋ :iz :niəli ɔl -ðɛə wəək s -dan bəi məʃijnərĭ :nauədeiz: in:sted əv dĭveləpĭŋ -ðɛə masls bəi þræʃĭŋ wĭð ə fleil ən mouĭŋ wĭð ə saið, ɔl -ðei :duw ĭz tə :wotʃ ə məʃijn ðət -daz ɔl -ðɛə wəək fə ðəm.

hiə wĭj aar ŏn ðə top ə ðə daunz. :whot ə məgnifĭsənt vjuw!; həu hai -aa wĭ :hiə ‵? ə:baut siks ŏ sevn :handrəd fijt əi sə:pous. :sou matʃ!: əi ʃud nt əv þɔt ĭt. wel ‵, jŭ :sij ‵, ðə houl kantrĭ :laiz :pritĭ hai: mai haus ĭz ə:baut fɔə :handrəd fijt ə-bav ðə sij. ðĭ ɛə :sijmz matʃ freʃə ap hiə ðən daun ĭn ðə vælĭ. :ou ᵛjes; ĭt s matʃ draiə ‵, ən jŭ dount -get -ðæt smel əv dĭkeiĭŋ vedʒĭ·teiʃən ən stægnənt wɔtə; əi v ɔfn :þɔt əv :bildĭŋ ə haus :ap hiə. sam dei -ðei l :bild ə big hŏutel :præps. ðæt s not :verĭ laiklĭ; ʃəl wĭj si daun :hiər ən rest ə :bit? nou þæŋk jŭ. ou ‵, əi fəgot; let s -gou on -ðen; əi l teik jŭ bæk bə məi feivrĭt raf roud: jŭ :get ə fain :vjuw ə ðə muər ɔl ðə wei.

4.

əi ·tould jŭ gædbrŭk əd kɔl əz :suwn əz ĭj həəd jŭ wə :hiə; :who d jŭ þiŋk əv ĭm ‵? wel ‵, ĭj z -wan ə ðə mŏust briljənt ən fæsĭneitĭŋ :men əi evə -keim əkrɔs: hĭz :flou əv tɔk s ·wandəfl: hĭj l haadlĭ -let jŭ -get ə wəəd ĭn edʒweiz; huw wəz :ðæt -jaŋ :felŏu ĭj :brɔt wĭð ĭm ‵? — klerĭkl ‵, əv kɔs. jes ‵, -ðæt wəz belŏu ‵, ðə njuw kjuərĭt; :who d jŭ :þiŋk əv ·him ‵? ŏu, ĭj :sijmz ə -verĭ pleznt -jaŋ :felŏu ′—verĭ zeləs əbəut ĭz pærĭʃ wəək ′; bət ĭt s ə pitĭ ĭj z sŏu an·nesĭsərĭlĭ oilĭ ĭn :mænə; :iz ĭj ən oksfəd :mæn? nou ‵, kiŋz kolĭdʒ. kiŋz :kolĭdʒ landən? jes.

əi sə:pouz wĭj ɔt tə rĭtəən :gædbrŭks ·kɔl :suwn ‵— :whai d

jŭ laaf ˋ? ou naþĭŋ ˋ— ɔl rait ˊ: :let s -meik ɗĭ ĭksperĭmənt. whai ĭksperĭmənt ˋ? : :iz ĭt sətʃ ə difĭklt ŏ deinʒərəs entəprəiz ? ·juw ʃl sij. d jŭ mijn ĭj wount bĭj ət houm ? ɗæt dĭpendz ŏn whŏt jŭ ^mijn bəi -bijĭŋ ət :houm. əi dount andə·stænd. ·juw ʃl sij.

ɗɛə z -wan ə jŏ dʒəəmən bændz ˋ— :whai əi bĭlijv ĭt s ɗə veri -seim :wan əi sɔ :laast jiə ət ɗə :fut əv snoudn ˋ—ɗə verĭ :laas :pleis əi ʃəd əv ĭkspektĭd tə mijt -wan ! ən nau ĭt -təənz ap ə-gen ĭn ə stil :mɔr autəɗəwei pleis ! jes ˊ: ɗə seim əidentĭkl tjuwnz ; ənd əi nou -ɗæt spotĭfeist :felŏu wĭ ɗə bluw kæp əz wel əz :if ĭj wə məi oun braɗə. ĭt s not ə bæd laif fə :ɗouz :felŏuz ˊ: -ɗei -hæv ə pleznt holĭdĭ ɔl ɗə samə ˊ; ənd ĭn ɗə wintə -ɗei setl dəun :kamftəblĭ ĭn sam laadʒ taun ; :if jŭ wə tə gŏu tə baaþ ŏ tʃeltn-əm ĭn ɗə wintə, əi dɛəsei jŭw d -hæv ɗə :pleʒər əv :sijĭŋ jŏ spotĭfeist frend əgen ˋ— -ɗei səətnlĭ ər ə ·wandəfl pijpl. jes ˊ, -ɗei :sijm tə bĭ puʃĭŋ -ɗɛə wei ·evrĭwhɛə : ɔl ɗə ·weitəz ə dʒəəmənz nauədeiz. ɗə weitər ĭn ɗə hŏutel ət ·stokbrĭdʒ wəz ə dʒəəmən. əi aast ĭm ĭf -ɗei d :got -enĭ təbækŏu tə :meik sigə·rets wĭɗ ˋ, ən ĭj :brɔt mĭj ə dʒəəmən sĭgaar insted ; ĭt riəlĭ :woz nt bæd. hĭj sed ĭj d pəsweidĭd ɗə mænĭdʒə tə get ɗəm insted ə ɗə bijslĭ imĭ·teiʃən həvænəz -ɗei juws tə kijp. əi ʃəd :kɔl -ɗæt aut ə ɗə fraiĭŋ-pæn :intə ɗə ^faiə. əi m ᵛounli telĭŋ jŭ whŏt ·hij :tould mij ˊ. ɔl rait ˊ, gou on ˊ. wel ˋ, ɗis jaŋ felŏu tould mĭ ĭj wəz ɗə san əv ə treidzmən ĭn :sam -litl dʒəəmən taun. hĭj d kam ŏuvə :hiər əz ə weitə tə ləən iŋglĭʃ. hĭj :sed ə gud :menĭ rĭspektəbl dʒəəmənz dĭd ɗə seim ˋ— :wel edjŭkeitĭd :felŏuz tuw. :when -ɗei v ləənt ĭ:naf iŋglĭʃ, -ɗei gou bæk tə dʒəəmənĭ ən -get gud pleisĭz þrŭw :nouĭŋ iŋglĭʃ. ɗis :jaŋ felŏu ĭkspektĭd tə -get ə gud pleis ĭn ə ·bæŋk -when ĭj went bæk ˋ— ət :lijst ĭj sed sŏu. ĭt :sijmz -ɗei ɔfn -meik ə gud þiŋ əv ĭt bĭsaidz :ləənĭŋ :iŋglĭʃ fə naþĭŋ : -ɗei dount -get matʃ ĭn ɗə -wei əv weidʒĭz′; bət ðə tips -kam tə sampþĭŋ ĭn ðə -kɔs əv ə jiər ŏ :tuw.

wel ˋ, d jŭ -fijl ·betə fə kɔlĭŋ ŏn gædbruk? :wel, wĭj -hæv ət lijst ðə sætĭs·fækʃən əv -hævĭŋ dan ðə kərekt þiŋ. bət :who d jŭ þiŋk əv əuə rĭ·sepʃən ˋ? əi kənfes əi -fijl :raaðə mistĭfəid: juw riŋ ðə bel, ənd ət ðə þəəd :rĭŋ ə :samwhŏt dĭsrepjŭtəbl-lukĭŋ hausmeid ə:piəz; juw aask ĭf mĭstə ·gædbruk s ət :houm, ən rĭ:sijv ən an·hezĭteitĭŋ aansər ĭn ðĭ əfəəmətĭv; wĭə ʃoun ĭntə :whot əi əsjuwm tə bĭj ðə greit :mænz praivĭt den, sæŋktəm, ŏ stadĭ ˋ—whŏtevə jŭ :laik tə kɔl ĭt; :ðen -aaftər ə prəloŋd æbsəns, ʃĭj rĭtəənz ˋ, ən ĭnfɔmz əs ʃĭj wəz mĭsteikn: mĭstə gædbruk ĭz ·not ət houm; juw kaamlĭ aask, ':did ĭj :tel jŭ tə sei sŏu ĭm·self?; :whɛərəpŏn ðə gəəl :bləəts aut 'jes səˋ,' ənd ĭz :ĭmijdʒətlĭ ouvə·whelmd wĭð kənfjuwʒən; wij :wɔk aut, ən hiə wĭ aar ŏn əuə :wei tə ðə daunz ˋ—:æm əi tŭ andə·stænd ðət :ðis ĭz ĭz juwʒŭəl :stail əv rĭsijvĭŋ vizĭtəz? ðæt dĭpendz ŏn huw ðə vizitər ^iz. d juw -mijn tə :sei jŭ :gou ŏn əsouʃĭeitĭŋ wĭð ə :mæn ŭw bĭ:heivz ĭn ðæt -wei? ˇai :dount ə:souʃĭeit wĭð ĭm: ·hij ə:souʃĭeits wĭð ^mij; bət əi kənfes ĭt :juws tŭ ægrəveit mĭj kənsidrəblĭ ət :fəəst. jŭw məs :nou ðət ĭt wəz ĭntaiəlĭ þrŭw gædbruk ðət əi :keim ən :setld hiə ˋ—ĭn :fækt ĭj pŭt ə :gudĭjl əv frendlĭ ·preʃər ŏn mĭj. wel ˋ, wĭj hæd nt bĭjn ĭn ðə haus tuw deiz, -when gædbruk kɔld wĭð tuw əv ĭz dɔtəz. ĭt wəz raaðər ɔkwəd, əz wĭj hæd nt gŏt ɔl əuə fəənĭtʃər ĭn: wĭj wər ĭn ə mŏust ɔfl -steit əv kənfjuwʒən ˋ—ðə wəz haadlĭ rum tə si daun. həuevə, wĭj mænĭdʒd tə :get þĭŋz ·streit ə lĭtl ən tə :giv ðəm səm tij. hĭj wəz verĭ pleznt′ —tɔkt əwei fər əbaut ·tuw auəz. həu:evə məi waif tŭk ðə greitĭst dĭslaik tŭ ĭm ˋ, ənd ijvn :went sŏu faar əz tə sei ĭj wəz nou dʒentlmən ˋ, whĭtʃ :sijmd raaðə bould ˋ, kən:sidrĭŋ ĭj bousts ðət ĭz fæmĭlĭ z :bijn ĭn ðĭs :pleis fə məə ðən faiv :handrəd jiəz. tuw deiz aaftə, tŭ əuə səprais, ĭj :sent ĭz waif tə :kɔl ŏn əs. wĭj :raaðə pitĭd -əə: ʃĭj did nt :sijm :verĭ hæpĭ əbəut ĭt. əz suwn əz wĭj d gŏt ðə ·haus ĭn ɔdə, wĭj rĭtəənd :ðijz kɔlz. wĭj wə tould ðət :naiðə mistə nŏ misĭz :gædbruk wər ət houm. ə fɔtnəit aaftə gædbruk kɔld wĭð jaŋ belŏu, ðə kjuərĭt. nekst wijk əi kɔld bəi məiself ˎ, ən wəz tould ĭj wəz not ət houm. tuw manþs aaftər ĭj kɔld wĭð tʃæpmən. -ðæt wəz ə:baut faiv :jiəz əgou. əi nau :kɔl fə ðə þəəd :taim ˎ—wĭð juw ˎ—ən fə ðə þəəd :taim :faind ĭj z not ət houm. whai ˎ, ðə :felŏu mas bĭj ə ·regjələ ·kæd!—ŏr els reivĭŋ mædˊ. ^ou nŏu: hĭj z not ə bæd :felŏu ĭn ĭz wei ˊ; əi :raaðə ^laik ĭm: hĭj z ðə fainĭst spesĭmĭn əi evə njuw əv ðə pjuəlĭ ĭmpalsĭv temprəmənt kəm:baind wĭð atəlĭ an·konʃəs egŏtĭzm. wel ˎ, əi nevə wəz sŏu kəmplijtlĭ :teikn in ĭn məi laif; əi þɔt ĭj wəz ə ·þarəlĭ gud felŏu: hĭj wəz sou ^frendlĭ, ən :sijmd sŏu æŋʃəs tə -meik məi əkweintəns. jes ˎ, bət :if jŭ þiŋk əv ĭt, ĭj :nevə wans :ɔfəd jŭ -enĭ kaindnĭs ŏ hospĭ·tælĭtĭ; :ijvn -when jŭ :sed jŭw d laik tə :sij -ðæt ·bijm ĭn ĭz haus wĭð :whot ĭj :kɔlz ðə ruwnĭk ĭnskripʃən ŏn ĭt, hĭj nevə :sed ĭj houpt jŭw d -kam raund ən sij ĭt ˎ, ŏr :enĭþĭŋ ə ðæt :sɔt; ən :when jŭ :sed jŭ wə :fond əv fiʃĭŋ, hĭj nevər :ɔfəd tə :let jŭ :fiʃ ĭn ĭz strijm, :ðou ĭj nevə :fiʃĭz ĭmself, ən ðə :fiʃĭŋ əd :riəlĭ bij ĭmpruwvd ĭf :sam ə ðə big fiʃ wə :teikn aut. bət ·whai wəz ĭj sŏu æŋʃəs tə -meik məi əkweintəns -ðen ˎ?—əi kaant meik ĭt aut. kjuərĭ;osĭtĭ ˎ—naþĭŋ els: hĭj d həəd əv jŭ, ən :wontĭd tə :sij whot jŭ wə laik. əz suwn əz ĭz kjuəri:osĭtĭ wəz sætĭsfəid, hĭj :wontĭd tə -get rid əv jŭ ˎ, ən -hæv nou -mɔə boðə wĭð jŭ. kənfaund ðə :felŏu!; əi ʃəd :laik tə kik ĭm! ðæt wŭd nt :duw enĭ gudˊ: ĭj wud nt andə·stænd whŏt jŭ ment; ən bĭsaidz ˎ, ĭj d bĭ :raaðər ən ɔkwəd ·kastəmə tə kik: hĭj z an·komənlĭ taf. bət əi wandə ðə pijpl əbəut :hiə ·stænd -ðæt -kəind əv :þĭŋ! -ðei :kaant ^help ðəm-selvz: :whot kən jŭ sei tŭ ə :mæn ŭw livz ĭn satʃ ə :haus əz ðæt ˎ? jŭw v nou əidiə :hau ðə ruwnĭk ĭnskripʃən ouvər·ɔz ðəm. əv :kɔs ĭt iz nt ə :ruwnĭk ĭn:skripʃən ətɔl', bət ðæt daz nt -meik -enĭ difrəns; bət siəriəslĭ', ĭt s ə greit mĭsfɔtʃən fər ə :mæn ə ðæt :kærĭktə tə bĭ :eibl tə :plei traut ə-maŋ ðə minŏuz wĭð ĭmpjuwnĭtĭ. hĭj :sijmz tə gŏu ŏn ðĭ ĭgzækt opəzĭt əv ðə mæksĭm noubles ŏblijʒ. prĭsaislĭ sŏu; ənd :ɔl ðə :whail ĭj dĭvautlĭ bĭlijvz ĭj z :duwĭŋ iz best tə kijp ɔf ðĭ ĭmpendĭŋ revə·ljuwʃən.

ə reilwei ĭkskəəʃən.

:who də jŭ duw wĭð jə-self ŏn sandĭz'?: jŭw məs faind ĭt -raaðə dal :livĭŋ hiər ɔl bə jŏself. ou', :when ĭt s fain, əi dʒenrəlĭ gŏu :aut əv taun ŏn :sandĭ: əi -teik ðə trein ə:baut ten ŏ twelv mailz :aut əv landən, ən wɔk aut tə sam pleis -whɛər əi kən -get ə trein bæk. ĭt s -raaðər ɔkwəd :samtəimz bĭ:koz ðər ə sŏu fjuw treinz ŏn sandĭz. əi rĭmembə wans əi wəz aut fə ðə dei wĭð ə lot ə felŏuz, ən wĭj mist əuə wei :saməu -getĭŋ tə ðə steiʃən'—əi raaðə þiŋk wĭj went tə ðə ·roŋ steiʃən', ən sou -hæd tə :gou tə ðĭ aðə -wan'—:enĭhəu, dʒest əz wĭj -keim :ap tə ðə steiʃən, ðə potə ʃat ðə dor ĭn əuə feisĭz. hĭj məit ijzl-ĭ əv -let əs in, fə ðə trein did nt staat tĭl tuw :minĭts aaftə: əi sə:pouz ĭj ment ĭt əz ə :kaind əv præktĭkl dʒouk. enĭhəu, ĭt wəz ðə laas trein', ən ðə wəz :nou help fr ĭt: wĭj hæd tə wɔk houm. :hau faa wəz ĭt'? fɔtijn mailz. wel', ðæt :woz nt matʃ. ^nou, bət wĭj d ɔl·redĭ :wɔkt niəlĭ þəətĭ mailz. əi did nt -get houm tĭl niə wan', ən sam əv əs -hæd ·fəəðə tə gou. wan :jaŋ :felŏu wəz kəmplijtlĭ :nokt ap: əi bĭ:lijv ĭj :hæd tə :lai ĭn ·bed fər ə dei ŏ :tuw. ai wəz :nan ðə wəəs fər ĭt. wel', whitʃ ·trein ʃə wĭj gou bəi tə:morŏu'; ðəz wan ət nain, ənd ənaðə ət haaf :paas twelv ŏ twelv :þəətĭ faiv —əi fəget whitʃ. wĭj d betə -teik ðə nain -wan', ĭf ĭt iz nt tŭw əəlĭ fə jŭw. ĭt ·iz raaðər əəlĭ; bət ĭt kaan bĭ helpt: əi məs -teik ə kæb :if əi m :not ap ĭn :taim. -ðen ĭt s setld ðət wĭə tə mijt ət ðə steiʃən ət nain ei em tə:morŏu mɔnĭŋ\? jes\, ĭk:sept ðət ðə z :nou ə:keiʒən tə :sei mɔnĭŋ twais ouvə. twais ouvə/: :who də jŭ mijn\? :whai jŭ -sed ei em ən təmorŏu mɔnĭŋ: ei em ən mɔnĭŋ :mijn ĭgzæktlĭ ðə seim þiŋ, ĭk:sept ðət wan z ·lætĭn ən ðĭ aðəz ·iŋglĭʃ. :hau d jŭ -meik aut ðət ei em z lætĭn\?: əi doun :þiŋk ən einʃənt roumən əd andə·stænd jŭ ĭf jŭ -sed ei em/: hĭj d andə:stænd æntĭ ᵛmĭ·ridjem :kwik ĭnaf, bət not ei em. jŏ tuw kritĭkl. wel\, juw bĭgæn ĭt.

hiə jŭ aa/!; :hau :lɔŋ əv jŭ bijn hĭə\? əbaut tuw minĭts. :whot s ðə taim\?: əi m əfreid məi ·wotʃ ĭz rɔŋ. ĭt s ĭgzæktlĭ eit minĭts tə nain. -ðen əi m faiv :minĭts faast; məi wotʃ stopt ət haaf :paas siks ðĭs mɔnĭŋ\—əi sə:pouz əi fəgot tə :waind ĭt ap :laas :nait\—ənd əi məst əv set ĭt rɔŋ. wel\, ĭt s betə ðən -hævĭŋ ĭt slou. aa, -ðɛə z ðə tikĭtpleis :oupn: ʃl əi -get jɔə :tikĭt tuw? jes\, ĭf jŭ wil/. whitʃ klaas\? :ou, seknd əi sə:pouz. :whot s ðə :gud əv :gouĭŋ sekənd\?: ·ai ɔlwĭz gŏu fəəst ŏ þəəd\—:dʒenrəlĭ þəəd: ðə laas taim əi :trævld seknd ðə wə tuw flaŋkĭz ən ə leidĭzmeid ĭn ðə :kærĭdʒ, ənd ət ðə neks :steiʃən ðə wəz ə raʃ əv betĭŋmen ən kaadʃaapəz, ɔl mɔr ŏ :les draŋk. sŏu əi got aut ət ðə neks steiʃən ən got ĭntŭ ə þəəd smoukĭŋ\—səm verĭ :gud felŏuz in ĭt. wel -ðen :let ĭt bĭ þəəd: ĭt s ɔl ðə :seim tə mij. əi sə:pouz wĭj d betə :not :teik rĭtəənz; wĭj ·mei wont tə kam bæk -sam aðə wei. jes\, betə :teik siŋgl. tuw þəədz daunfəd! rĭtəən/? nou\, siŋgl. hiə z jŏ tikĭt/; əi sə:pouz ðis ĭz ðə :said fə daunfəd. wel, -ðei :sijm tə bĭ ɔl -gouĭŋ :ouvə tə ðĭ aðə :said. əi l aask -ðæt pɔtə; jes\, ĭt s ðĭ aðə :plætfɔm: wĭj məs :gou ə-krɔs ðə bridʒ. əi -raaðə laik ðĭs\, -hævĭŋ ə kærĭdʒ ɔl tŭ əuəselvz. ·hal·lou, :whɛə z məi ambə·relə\?; əi məs gŏu ən luk fŏr ĭt. jŭw d betə :luk ʃaap/: əuə taim z ap\—ðə trein ɔt tŭ əv

·staatĭd bəi ðis təim. hiər ĭt iz!: əi d :left ĭt ĭn ðə bukĭŋɔfĭs. whai də -ðei :kɔl ĭt ·bukĭŋɔfĭs\? ĭt :kamz frəm ðĭ ould ·koutʃĭŋ deiz -when -ðei :juws tŭ entə jŏ neim ĭn ə buk. ^ou -jes, ən ðæt s whəi -ðei tɔk əv ·bukĭŋ fər ə steiʃən in-sted əv :teikĭŋ ə tikĭt fŏr ĭt. ĭn ðə seim wei -ðei juws tə kɔl ðə kærĭdʒĭz ·koutʃiz: ðə ·fəəst reilwei kærĭdʒĭz wər ĭgzækt imĭ·teiʃənz ə ðĭ ould ·steidʒ ·koutʃiz. nau wĭər ɔf ət -laast!

ĭz ðis əuə steiʃən? nou\, wĭj dount ·stop :hiə: ðis ĭz ə faas :trein. hau -menĭ :mɔ steiʃənz hæv wĭj\? tuw\, əi :þiŋk. whot steiʃən z ðis\? ĭt s -sam njuw :steiʃən: ·fɔtĭskjŭw ·paak əi þiŋk -ðei kɔl ĭt. hiə wĭj aa/: ðis ĭz daunfəd. əi m glæd tə hiər ĭt: əi ʃəl bĭ glæd tə -get aut, ən stretʃ məi ·legz ə :litl. :whot s ðə mætə\? əi :þɔt əi d lɔst məi ·tikĭt; əi -hæd ĭt ĭn məi hænd -ɔl ðə :taim; bət :whεə z məi ambə·relə\? whŏt əv jŭ lɔst ĭt. ə·gen/? əi -mast əv :left ĭt ĭn ðə trein. ʃəl wĭj gŏu bæk fŏr ĭt\? ĭt s tuw leit nau/: ðə trein z -gɔn on. wel, wĭj l :meik -ap əuə maindz tə :kam :bæk hiə; -præps -ðei l əv faund ĭt ĭn ðə kærĭdʒ. wĭj mait əz -wel əv -teikn rĭtəəntikĭts -aaftər ɔl. ĭt daz nt mætə/: wĭj ʃud nt əv ·seivd -enĭþĭŋ bəi ĭt/.

ət ðə sij said.

:hæd nt jŭ :betə -get ap -nau/?: ĭt s -getĭŋ leit. :hæv jŭ :ɔdəd brekfəst? jes. ðæt s :ɔl rait; əi l bĭ daun ĭn ten minĭts. :when wĭj v -hæd brekfəst, wĭj l gŏu aut n :luk fə lodʒĭŋz: əi m əfreid ðĭs hŏutel l bĭ :raaðər ĭkspensĭv.

ə jŭ redĭ? əi ʃl bĭ :redĭ ĭn ə minĭt: əi v ounlĭ :got tə -get məi buwts ŏn. əi :wandə :whitʃ ĭz ðə wei tə ðə sij; ðis məs :bij ĭt\, əi :þiŋk. ðεə z ðə sij/—whəi wĭə kwait klous tŭ ĭt!

-ðɛər ə səm bouts; :who də jŭ :sei tŭ ə rou \?; seilĭŋbouts tuw; -let s :gou fər ə seil! wĭj :hæv nt taim :nau: wĭj v got tə :faind lodʒĭŋz; wĭj mei əz -wel -hæv ə beið ðŏu ′: ·ðæt wount teik loŋ. ᵛai ʃaant beið: ĭt s tuw kould fə mĭj. wel \, luk hiə \—ai l beið, ən juw ʃl gŏu ən :luk fə lodʒĭŋz \—juw andə·stænd ðæt :kaind əv :þiŋ betə ðən ai dŭw; jŭw l faind m̩ĭj hiə -when jŭ :kam bæk.

:hau dĭd jŭ :laik jŏ beið \?: wəz ðə wɔtə wɔm? nevə -hæd ə betə beið ĭn məi laif; ðə wɔtə wəz raaðə kould, bət əi dount :maind ðæt. wel, əi v got səm rumz fŏr əs ĭn ðæt lĭtl haus -ap :ðɛər ŏn ðə terĭs; þəətĭ :ʃilĭŋz ə wijk, nou ekstrəz, nou -aðə lodʒəz, nou tʃuldrən, pəəfĭkt kwaiət insəid n autsəid ðə haus. jŭw v bĭjn ə loŋ :taim əbaut ĭt ′. jes \, əi kud nt -get əwei frəm ðĭ ould wumən \—ʃĭj tɔkt sŏu; ʃĭj :sez wĭj kən kam in when:evə wĭj laik: ðə rumz ər ɔl redĭ. -ðen wĭj l :gou -ðɛər ĭn ðĭ aaftə·nuwn. əi houp ðə :pijpl ər onĭst: əi kaan ·bɛə tə bĭ ɔl:wĭz səspektĭŋ pĭjpl. d jŭw rĭmembə ·smiþs stɔrĭz əv ĭz ĭkspiərĭənsĭz ĭn sijsəid lodʒĭŋz? nou \, :whot woz ĭt \?. wel \, ŏn wan ə:keiʒən ĭj -æd dauts ə ðĭ onĭstĭ əv ĭz lænleidĭ \, sŏu ĭj bɔt ə paund əv tij, ən pŭt haaf əv ĭt ĭn ðə kabəd; ðĭ aðə :haaf :paund ĭj kept lokt ap ĭn ĭz raitĭŋdesk \, ən :meid ĭz tij wĭð ĭt \—hĭj did nt :juwz ðə tij ĭn ðə kabəd ətɔl. wel \, ət ðĭ end əv ə fɔtnəit hĭz lænleidĭ :keim tŭ ĭm tŭ rĭmaind ĭm ðət ĭz tij wəz niəlĭ ɔl dan \, ən tŭ aask ĭf ʃĭj ʃud nt -get səm mɔə fŏr ĭm. sou ĭj :sed '^ou :misĭz braun \—ŏ whŏtevər -əə neim wŏz ′—' əi v :meid ᵛmai tij laast loŋgə ðən jɔəz: əi v stil gŏt ə kwɔtər əv ə paund left.' ənaðə təim ĭj borŏud səm dĭkæntəz əv ĭz lænleidĭ tə :put səm wain ĭn \, əz ĭj :sed; bət ĭnsted ə ðæt ĭj kept ðə wain ĭn ĭz pɔt·mæntŏu \, ən taid ðə neks ə ðə dĭkæntəz tə ðə kijhoul ə ðə kabəd dɔə \, sŏu ðət :when ʃĭj oupnd ĭt tə :get ət ðə wain, ʃĭj :puld ðĭ emtĭ dĭkæntəz aut ə ðə kabəd :on tə ðə flɔə \, ən -ðei wə smæʃt :ɔl tə pijsĭz. əi þiŋk smiþ :mast əv bĭjn -raaðər an·fɔtʃənĭt ĭn ðə :pijpl ĭj lodʒd wĭð—ᵛai v ɔlwĭz :faund ðəm onĭst i:naf. :præps :ðijz stɔrĭz· ər ĭz oun ĭnvenʃən. -ðæt s not ətɔl an·laiklĭ.

ai sei, əi fĭjl ɔfl-ĭ leizĭ :aaftə məi beið ən ðæt gud lanʃ -ðei geiv əs ət ðĭ ŏutel ′; əi ʃəd bĭ ɔfl-ĭ greitfl ĭf juw d gŏu bæk tə ðĭ ŏutel, ən sij əbəut muwvĭŋ əuə þiŋz ; ən jŭ məit ɔdə tij ət ðə seim taim ‵—əi səpouz wĭj ʃl hæv tə gŏu in fər əəlĭ dinər ən faivəklok ŏ siksəklok tij ‵—ən tel mĭsĭz whotsəneim tə :get ə :pot əv raazbrĭ dʒæm ‵, ən səm ʃrimps ‵—əi hæv nt -hæd ə ʃrimp tij fər evə sŏu :loŋ ‵, not sĭns əi :juws tə todl ə-krɔs grinĭdʒ paak wĭð məi nəəs ‵—ŏ betə stil səm prɔnz ; jes ‵, tel əə tə -get səm prɔnz. ĭt s raaðə kuwl əv mĭj :putĭŋ evrĭþiŋ ŏn juw ləik ðis, bət əi ·nou jŭ doun maind ′. wel ‵, əi promĭst jŏ maðər əi d :luk aaftə jŭ, ən sij ðət jŭ did nt ijt enĭþiŋ ðət disə·grijd wĭð jŭ ; əi doun :nou whot ʃĭj d sei tə raazbrĭ dʒæm ən ʃrimps ðŏu.

:ou, hiə jŭ aar ; əi kud nt faind jŭ : əi v setld evrĭþiŋ ət nambə faiv. həv jŭ ɔdəd tij ? jes ‵, ət haaf :paas faiv ; ʃĭj :sez prɔnz ə not tə bĭ got ; ʃĭj l trai ən -get səm ʃrimps, bət evrĭþiŋ ĭn ðə :wei əv fiʃ :gets sent ap tə landən ‵, sŏu jŭ kaaŋ get -enĭ an:les jŭ luk ʃaap. ðæt rĭmaindz mĭj : huw d jŭ :þiŋk əi sɔ :dʒes :nau ‵ ? huw ‵ ? ʃaap ən tævĭstŏk ; -ðei keim daun ðə dei bĭ-fɔə jestədĭ ‵, whĭtʃ hæpnd tə bĭ bæŋk holĭdĭ. ʃaap s ĭn ə greit reidʒ əbəut ĭt : :sez ĭj ·heits ðə :pleis, ən l nevə -kam hiər əgen. əi wandər ĭj evə ^keim :hiə ‵—ə misn·þropĭkl, an·souʃəl :felŏu ləik ðæt. ŏu ĭt wəz ɔl ·tævĭstoks :duwĭŋ : hij dĭlaits ĭn ə kraud ‵, ən ðə mɔə raudĭ ən kædĭʃ ðə kraud iz, ðə mor ĭj z plijzd ‵—hĭj :sez ĭj -æz an·baundĭd feiþ ĭn ðə fjuwtʃər əv ðə britĭʃ dĭmokrəsĭ. ĭt s kjuərĭəs ðət ðouz tuw ʃəd bĭj sətʃ gud frendz ‵, ən :jet -ðei nevə :sijm tŭ əgrij : tævĭstok əbjuwzĭz ʃaap, ən :sez ĭj z ə retʃĭd :ould tɔrĭ əristəkræt ‵, ən ʃaap kɔlz tævĭstok ə sjuwpə·fiʃəl, ʃælŏumaindĭd optĭmĭst. ðə kjuərĭəs :þiŋ iz ðət tævĭstok s :riəlĭ matʃ :mɔr əv ən əristəkræt ðən ʃaap: əi bĭ:lijv ĭj bĭ:loŋz tŭ ə verĭ :gud fæmĭlĭ. ĭt wəz əmjuwzĭŋ tə :hiə ʃaap :tɔkĭŋ əv -ðɛər ədvenʃəz ŏn mandĭ: həu tævĭstok -meid frendz wĭð evrĭbodĭ ', ən tʃaaft ðə gəəlz ', tĭl ət :laast ĭj :rauzd ðə dʒeləsĭ əv :ðɛə jaŋ men ', ən -ðei :hæd regjələlĭ tə ·fait -ðɛə wei þrŭw ə sijðĭŋ mæs əv ærĭz: jŭw kən ĭmædʒĭn həu pleznt :ɔl ðis wŏz fə ʃaap ', ə :mæn ŭw stændz ŏn ĭz dignĭtĭ ', ən heits fəmilĭ·ærĭtĭ; ʃaap :sez ðə houl bijtʃ wəz kavəd wĭð orĭnʒpijl ən grijzĭ peipə ðə neks dei; hĭj :sez tævĭstok stil rĭ:teinz ĭz bĭlijf ĭn ðə fjuwtʃər əv britĭʃ dĭmokrəsĭ. əi ʃəd :laik tə sij tævĭstok '—:aa -ðei gŏuĭŋ tə stop :hiə loŋ? -ðɛə :gouĭŋ ə:wei təmorŏu; bət əi aast ðəm tə :kam :in ən :hæv ·tij wĭð əs ðis ijvnĭŋ. ðæt s rait: :when dĭd ju :tel ðəm tə kam '? əbaut faiv. wel -ðen ', wĭj d betə bĭ :gouĭŋ bæk ', ŏ -ðei l bĭ -ðɛə bĭfɔr əs.

edʒŭ·keiʃən.

:whot ə jŏ :vjuwz ŏn ðə :sabdʒĭkt əv edʒŭ·keiʃən '?—əi ʃəd bĭ glæd tə hiə ðəm. wel ', -ðɛə verĭ :suwn steitĭd: əi hæv nt -enĭ ətɔl. jŭ ʃuəlĭ doun mijn tə sei ðət jŭw v nevə gĭvn ə moumĭnts þɔt tə ðə moust ĭmpɔtnt fæktər ĭn ðə fjuwtʃə dĭveləpmənt ə ðə hjuwmən reis? ˋsə:pouz jŭw -hæd tʃuldrən əv jŏr oun '—d jŭw mijn tə sei ðət -ðɛə fizĭkl, morəl ən intĭ·lektʃŭəl dĭveləpmənt əd bĭj ə :mætər əv æbsəljŭwt ĭndifrəns :tuw jŭ? əv :kɔs əi wiʃ tə :sij məi :felŏu krijtʃəz helþi ĭn bodĭ ən maind :raaðə ðən wijk ən viʃəs '—:whot əi :mijn tə sei ĭz ðət əi doun :þiŋk edʒŭ·keiʃən -æz :matʃ tə duw wĭð ĭt: ĭt s nou juws tijtʃĭŋ mərælĭtĭ ən ðə lɔz əv helþ ət skuwl ĭf ðə tʃuldrənz houmlaif s an·helþi ən viʃəs; ən nou ə:maunt əv kræmĭŋ ðə maind l -meik ə stjuwpĭd :boi klevəˋ—ĭn :fækt ĭt l -hæv ĭgzæktlĭ ðĭ ·opəzĭt ĭfekt. mai faaðə wəz ə doktrĭ·nɛə dʒes ləik juw—. əi m ·not ə doktrĭ·nɛə. wel ˋ, :enihəu hĭj -æd stroŋ vjuwz ŏn ðə :sabdʒĭkt əv edʒŭ·keiʃən: ·hiz əi:diə :woz ðət nou :hjuwmən :bijĭŋ z nætʃərəlĭ aidl ˋ, ən ðət ĭf jŭ wans :faind aut whŏt ijtʃ -wan -hæz ə speʃəl æptĭtjŭwd fŏə, ən set ðəm tŭ ĭt, -ðei l -gou on ə ðəmselvz. əi ·kwait əgrij wĭð ĭm: ðĭ ounlĭ ·difĭkltĭ ĭz tə :faind aut ðĭjz speʃəl ætrĭbjŭwtsˋ —əi :mijn æptĭtjŭwdz. prĭsaislĭ sŏu ˋ—mai faaðə þɔt ĭj d dĭskavəd ðət ·mai :speʃəl :æptĭtjŭwd wəz ðə :stadĭ əv iŋglĭʃ litrətʃə əv ðə sevntijnþ senʃərĭ. əz ðis wəz ĭz oun speʃəl hobĭ, hĭj wəz dĭlaitĭd wĭð ĭz dĭskavərĭ ˋ, ən meid mĭj :fijl ðə weit əv ĭt; ðə rĭzalt ĭz ðət əi -hæv ə pəəfĭkt heitrĭd əv litrətʃə ˋ—ðə :verĭ ·sait əv ə voljəm əv miltn ŏ kaulĭ ŏ dreitn -meiks mĭj il. jes ˋ, ðĭ ounlĭ :litrətʃə jŭ :sijm tŭ əprijʃieit ĭz ðə pelmel badʒĭt ən ðə fijld. kam ˋ, əi :rijd ðə mægə·zijnz :samtəimz ˊ. jŭ :mijn, jŭ :luk ət ðĭ ilə·streiʃənz ĭn haapə ˋ, ən :rijd ə gous-stɔrĭ :nau ən :ðen. ĭt l :præps reiz mĭ :samwhŏt ĭn jŏr əpinjən ĭf əi tel jŭ ðət əi riəlĭ tŭk ə :gudĭjl əv intərest ĭn edʒŭ·keiʃən tuw :jiəz əgou; əi :ijvn -went sŏu faar əz tŭ ɔdə həəbət spensər ŏn edʒŭ·keiʃən. ə frend əv məin hŭw z ən aadnt spensərəit wəz horəstrak ət məi sŭwpəfiʃəl :wei əv əproutʃĭŋ ðə sabdʒĭkt ˋ, ən :sed əi ɔt nt tə ·þiŋk əv :rijdĭŋ ðĭ edʒŭ·keiʃən ən:til əi d maastəd fəəst prinsĭplz. ðĭ end əv ĭt :woz ðət əi ĭnvestĭd ĭn ə kəmplijt set əv həəbət spensəz wəəks ˋ; bət ·an·fɔtʃənətlĭ əi stak faast ĭn ðə midl ə ðə fəəst tʃæptə əv fəəst prinsĭplz; sŏu əv :kɔs əi nevə gŏt tə ðĭ edʒŭ·keiʃən ətɔl. ðɛə -ðei aa ˊ—ðə houl siərĭz ˋ—kəmplijt wəəks əv həəbət spensə ˋ—:on ə ʃelf ɔl tə ðəmselvz: əi :hæd ĭt pŭt ap ŏn pəəpəs. wel, ðər ə sam :points ŏn whĭtʃ əi douŋ kwait əgrij wĭð spensə məiselfˋ—.

þæŋks ‵, əi d raaðə :not :hiər -enĭ kritĭsĭzmz tĭl əi v red ðə :buk məiself: əi dount wont tə ·baiəs məi maind ĭn enĭ :wei. əi m əfreid ĭt s moə wont əv intərest ĭn ðə sabdʒĭkt ðən lav əv ĭmpaaʃĭ·ælĭtĭ ′; bət əi kaant andə·stænd həu enĭwan ŭw z wans -teikn ən :intərest ĭn edʒŭ·keiʃən kən evə luwz ĭt.

:sins əi :sɔ jŭ laast, əi v ·red -ðæt :buk ŏn edʒŭ·keiʃən. ·whot buk ŏn edʒŭ·keiʃən ‵? həəbət spensəz; ĭt s :ɔl nonsəns əbəut jŏ hævĭŋ tə :rijd fəəst ·prinsəplz :fəəst. əi red ĭt þruw, ən andə·stud evrĭ wəəd: ĭt s :ɔl əz kliər əz kən bij. əi əgrij wĭð ɔl ĭj sez ‵, ĭspeʃəlĭ əbəut ·fizĭkl edʒŭ:keiʃən. whŏt əi ·speʃəlĭ ĭndʒoid ər ĭz hits ət ɔnə·mentl skoləʃĭp. hiə z ðə :pæsĭdʒ əi :mijn ′—peidʒ sevn·tijn: ':men ŭw d ·blaʃ :if :kɔt seiĭŋ iſĭ;dʒijnjə ĭn:sted əv iſĭdʒĭ·naiə, ŏr əd rĭzent əz ən ·insalt :enĭ impjŭ:teiʃən əv ignərəns rĭ:spektĭŋ ðə feibld leibəz əv ə feibld demĭgod, :ʃou not ðə slaitĭst ʃeim ĭn kən:fesĭŋ ðət -ðei dount :nou whɛə ðə jŭwsteikjən tjuwbz -aa ‵, :whot ə ðĭ ækʃənz ə ðə spainl kɔd ‵, :whot s ðə nɔml :reit əv pal·seiʃən ‵, ən :hau ðə ·laŋz ər ĭnfleitĭd ‵′—ən sou ŏn. bət ᵛai :nevə həəd ə ðə jŭwsteikjən tjuwbz, dĭd juw? əi kənfes əi d fəgotn :ɔl əbaut ðəm -when əi fəəst :red spensəz buk; sins ðen əi v got -ap məi fizĭ;olədʒĭ ə-gen. :wel ‵, whŏt aa -ðei -ðen ‵? əi m əʃeimd tə sei əi v fəgotn əgen. ðĭ ounlĭ :þiŋ ðət boðəz mĭj :iz, :wheðər ĭt s matʃ gud raitĭŋ əbəut edʒŭ·keiʃən. ĭt sijmz tə mij ðət ðə ·riəl difĭkltĭ :iz, not tə ·nou whŏt s rait, bət tə ·duw ĭt. :when əi wəz ə boi, əi wəz tould ouvər ən ouvər əgen ðət :if əi lei ŏn ðə wet graas, əi ʃəd :get ðə ruwmətizəm :when əi :got ouldə; ən nau əi -hæv ĭt regjələlĭ evrĭ wintə ‵—əi -hæd səm twinʒĭz ŏv ĭt laas nait. -nau əi doun nou ðət əi :evə ·kwestʃənd ðə :fækt ðət əi ʃəd -get ruwmətizəm ′—əi simplĭ did nt kɛə. ðə fækt iz, sam :pijpl ə bɔn pruwdnt, :dʒest əz aðəz ə bɔn reklĭs ən ĭmpalsĭv; ən jŭ kaant ·oltə -ðɛə neitʃə bəi prijtʃĭŋ tə ðəm. nou-wan evə səpouzd ðət edʒŭ·keiʃən əd wəək mirĭklz ′: ĭt s ĭnaf ðət ĭt givz :pijpl ðə tʃaans əv :duwĭŋ whŏt s rait ən rijzn-əbl. bĭsaidz \, jŭ fəget ðət ĭt s :paat ə ðə :biznĭs əv edʒŭ·keiʃən tə trein :pijpl tə hæbĭts əv fɔəsait n ·selfrĭ·streint. -ðæt s dʒest whŏt əi daut -wheðər ĭt kən duw. ət :enĭ -reit əi m səətn jŭw d əv bĭjn ə betə :mæn ĭn evrĭ rĭ:spekt, ĭf jŏ faaðər əd edʒŭkeitĭd jŭ ŏn spensəz prinsĭplz. :verĭ laiklĭ; bət əi m əfreid əi ʃəd əv bĭjn :raaðər ə ·prig \—əi ʃəd əv bĭjn ·tuw pəəfĭkt.

souʃəlĭzm.

hiə jŭ aar, -aaftər ɔl! glæd tə faind jŭ ət **houm.** :whot :meid ðəm sei jŭ wəə nt ət houm \? əi ·tould ðəm tə sei sŏu. əi ᵛsei, bət ĭz :ðis kənsistənt wĭ ðə prinsĭplz ən **kærĭktər** əv ə ridʒĭd morəlist? :wel jŭ -sij əi m ɔfl-ĭ bizĭ, ən əi dount wont tə -hæv ə :lot əv aidl feloŭz :kamĭŋ in -ɔl :dei, ən weistĭŋ məi taim wĭð gosĭp. :ou nonsəns \: :daʒ jŭ gud. bət jŭ səətnlĭ luk bizĭ: jŏ ·berĭd ĭn buks \—buks ŏn ðə teibl, buks ŏn ðə tʃɛəz, buks ŏn ðə flɔə, paild ap tə ðə sijlĭŋ! :let s luk ət əm. ·hal·lou, :whot s ðis \?—·eþiks əv ·souʃəlĭzm, kwĭn·tesns əv souʃəlĭzm, ·kætĭkĭzm əv souʃəlĭzm, ·primər əv souʃəlĭzm ′— :whot s :ɔl ðis \? ·hal·lou, :hiə z ə ʃilĭŋ ^ʃokə—ðæt s mɔr ĭn ·mai :lain \—lukĭŋ bæk \—əi þɔt jŭ dĭs·paizd hjuw konwĭ \? :whot -æz lukĭŋ bæk tə duw wĭð hjuw konwĭ \?—ĭt s ə souʃəlist ^rəmæns—:bai ən əmerĭkən \—·beləmĭ. əi ^sij, əi wəz kənfaundĭŋ ĭt wĭð ·kɔld bæk. bət whot s :ɔl ðĭs nonsəns əv souʃəlĭzm \?; jŭ doun :mijn tə :sei jŭw v :təənd ·souʃəlist? -ðæt s dʒest whŏt əi ·duw -mijn tə :sei; əi nau glɔrĭ ĭn ðə :neim əv souʃəlĭst əz :matʃ əz əi fɔməlĭ əb·hɔd ən dĭspaizd ĭt. -ðen əi sə:pouz jŭ :gou in fə houm ruwl :tuw \?

:ou, əi v -got ə loŋ -wei bĭjond houm ruwl ĭn ðə laas :tuw wijks : tə mij ə mæn ŭwz vjuwz ə baundĭd bəi houm ruwl iz nt matʃ :mɔr ədvaanst ðən ən ouldfæʃənd tɔrĭ. :wel ', jŭ ·aa :gouĭŋ əhed : jŏr ə mŏus promĭsĭŋ souʃəlĭst beibĭ ', kən:sidrĭŋ jŏr :ounli tuw :wijks ould ; bət hau əbəut ezə·terĭk ·badĭzm ən þĭj·osəfĭ ' ? : ə manþ ŏ :tuw əgou əi :riəlĭ wəz əfreid jŭ wə -gouĭŋ ·mæd :ouvər ĭt ləik puə ·snaip. :hau ·iz :puə snaip ' ? : əi :hæv nt həəd əv ĭm fər evə sŏu :loŋ. :ou ĭj z :niəlĭ rĭkavəd :nau ; hĭj z :teikn tə stæmpkəlektĭŋ '—ðə doktə sez ĭt l :bij ðə sæl·veiʃən ŏv im ', :if ĭj l :ounlĭ stik tŭ ĭt. ət preznt ĭj þiŋks əv naþĭŋ els : hĭj :sez ðə spirĭts mə ræp ɔl dei loŋ ən ɔl ·nait :tuw əz haad əz -ðei laik '—·hij daz nt :kɛər ə ·ræp fər əm. bət spirĭtræpĭŋ -æz naþĭŋ tə :duw wĭð þĭjosəfĭ '. :ou, əi ĭks:pekt ĭj z :got ə -litl mikst : jŭ :nou ĭj bĭ·gæn wĭð spirĭtʃŭəlĭzm, ənd :ounlĭ -went :ouvə tə þĭjosəfĭ bĭ:koz ĭj wəz nou gud əz ə ·mijdʒəm. :ðæt s laiklĭ ĭnaf ; ai :douŋ kɛə -matʃ əbaut ĭt ; əi v :dan wĭð bouþ ə ðəm '—əi :faund ðə houl þiŋ ən ĭnfəənl swindl. hau dĭd jŭ :kam tə :giv ĭt ap ' ? jŭ wər əz ful əv ĭnþuwzĭæzm əz kəd bij : jŭ tould mĭj siərĭəslĭ jŭ wə :gouĭŋ tə :bĭj ə ·tʃijlə ŏ ·tʃeilə ', ŏ whŏtevə jŭ kɔl ĭt ; ən ðət jŭ ĭkspektĭd tə bĭj ə ·guərŭ ĭn :kɔs əv taim, wĭð ðə tʃaans əv sam :dei bĭjĭŋ ə plænĭtrĭ spirĭt '—ə ·dæn ·tʃɔboun əi þiŋk jŭ kɔld ĭt. jŭ wontĭd ·mij tə :gou in fr ĭt tuw ; ən :when əi aast həu loŋ ĭt əd teik, jŭ :sed ə miljən əv iənz ; ən :when əi :aast hau -matʃ ən ·iən :woz, jŭ :sed ən ĭn·kælkjələblĭ loŋ piərĭəd '—·miljənz əv jiəz ; sŏu əi :geiv ap ðĭ əidiə '—whot :meid ·juw :giv ĭt ap ' ? :wel, əi doum :maind teliŋ jŭ '—ĭt l bĭj ə rĭlijf tə :meik ə klijn ·brest əv ĭt '—bət jŭ məs swɛə soləmlĭ not tə ·tel :enĭwan. əi ·swɛə. wel -ðen ', ĭt :keim əbaut ĭn ðis -wei. :when əi fəəst :þɔt əv dʒoinĭŋ ðə braanʃ lijg -ðei d :dʒest ĭstæblĭʃt -hiə, əi felt sam dauts -æz tə :wheðər əi wəz spirĭtʃŭəlĭ dĭveləpt ĭ:naf. bət əz :suwn əz bedlŏu '—

jŭw nou bedlŏu, ŭw mænĭdzəz ðə lijg -hiə ′—əz :suwn əz ĭj :faund əi :tuk ən intərest ĭn ðə :þiŋ, hĭj prest mĭj :verĭ wɔmlĭ tə dʒoin ðəm ‵—ĭn :fækt ĭj wontĭd mĭj tə :teik ən ouþ streit ɔf ‵, bĭ:fɔr əi riəlĭ :njuw enĭþĭŋ əbaut ĭt. hĭj :sed əi -hæd ə verĭ rĭmaakəbl spirĭtʃuəl dĭveləpmənt; ən whot plijzd mĭj moust əv ɔl, hĭj -sed ĭj :þɔt əi wəz ə fifþ raundə. :whot on əəþ s ðæt ‵? ; :ou, əi rĭmembə jŏ telĭŋ mĭj :ɔl əbaut ĭt: ĭt -hæz :samþĭŋ tə duw wĭ ðə plænĭtrĭ tʃein ‵, :hæz nt ĭt ‵—ijtʃ raund korĭ·spondĭŋ tŭ ə steidʒ ĭn ðə dĭveləpmənt ə ðə hjuwmən reis ‵? jes ‵, ðæt s əbaut ĭt ‵—əiv :ɔlmŏust fəgotn ĭt məi:self. ɔl əi rĭmembər :iz ðət ĭj meid aut ðət whəil ðə ·rest əv hjŭw:mænĭtĭ wə toilĭŋ peinfl-ĭ þrŭw -ðɛə fɔþ :raund, ai wəz :wan ə ðə fjuw tʃois spirĭts ŭw d :got ĭntə ðə ·fifþ :raund. :wel ‵, əi wəz dʒest ŏn ðə point əv dʒoinĭŋ ðəm, -when əi faund aut ĭj d :sed ĭgzæktlĭ ðə seim þiŋ tə ·bæblkəm ‵—juw :nou bæblkəm ′—fænsĭ :ðæt ʃælŏu :felŏu bæblkəm ə fifþ raundə ‵—ə :felŏu ŭw raits pouĭtrĭ ‵, ən pablĭʃiz ĭt ət ĭz oun ĭkspens ‵!

:nau kæn jŭ tel mĭj :whot ·iz souʃəlĭzm; əi kaaŋ -get enĭwan tə tel mĭ. ðə peipəz ə ful əv ĭt; bət nan ə ðəm tel jŭ :whot ĭt iz ‵—əi doum bl-ijv -ðei :nou ðəmselvz. samtəimz -ðei tel jŭ ĭt s ĭn ðĭ ɛə; ·ðæt :daz nt help mĭj :matʃ. ən ðen -ðei tel jŭ -wiər ·ɔl souʃəlists. əi ·juws tə :þiŋk ĭt wəz ə lot əv :felŏuz wontĭŋ tə -hæv evrĭþĭŋ ĭn komən bĭ:koz -ðei hævnt -got enĭþĭŋ ðəmselvz. :ðæt s ·komjŭnĭzm ‵—·kwait ə difrənt þiŋ. wel -ðen ‵, :whot ·iz souʃəlĭzm ‵? souʃəlĭzm ′—whai ‵, ĭt s ·souʃəlĭzm ‵—əi dount ĭgzæktlĭ :nou ·hau tə dĭfain ĭt ‵—ĭt s a :þiŋ jŭ məs ·fijl; :if jŭ hæv nt ðə souʃəlĭst instĭŋkt, ĭt s nou gud. jes ‵, bət ᵛai m souʃəl ĭ:naf ′: əi heit tə bĭj əloun :ijvn fə faiv minĭts; əi ijvn tɔk tə ðə mæn ðət kats məi hɛə ‵—bət əi douŋ kənsidə məi-self ə souʃəlĭst ′. əi :sed ·souʃəlĭst :instĭŋkt, not souʃəl :instĭŋkt ′. wel ‵, :whot s ðə difrəns; ðæt s whŏt əi wont tə nou. difrəns ′—:whai evrĭ :difrəns ĭn ðə wəəld: ðə z əz matʃ difrəns bĭ:twijn souʃəl ən souʃəlĭst əz ðər iz bĭ:twijn ·egŏuĭst ən ·egŏutĭst. :ou əi ^sij: jŭ mijn ðət ə souʃəlĭst s ən egŏutĭst :təənd insəid aut \—ə :sɔt əv ĭn·vəətĭd egŏutĭst. jes \, ðæt defĭ·niʃən əl :duw əz wel əz :enĭ aðə. bət luk hiə \, jŭw d :betə teik ðə kwĭntesns n ðə primə /—əi ʃaant :wont ðəm bæk bĭfɔə krisməs /—ən rijd ðəm; ðen jŭw l :nou whŏt souʃəlĭzm :iz. əi ĭkspekt bəi ðə taim əi :briŋ ðəm bæk jŭw l əv aut·groun :souʃəlĭzm, ən :gɔn on tə ·komjŭnĭzm \, ŏ ·naiĭlĭzm \, ən :ðen wəəkt jŏ :wei bæk tə ·ræŋk kən;səəvətĭzm. :if əi m kənvinst ə ðə lodʒĭkl nĭsesĭtĭ əv -satʃ ə step, əi ʃəl səəntnlĭ teik ĭt; məi soul obdʒĭkt ĭz ·truwþ. ðəz ·wan :gud :þiŋ ə:baut juw: jŭw l nevə :grou ould \, bi:koz jŭw l ɔlwĭz -hæv sam njuw fæd \—sam :njuw ·hobĭ tə :raid; jŭw l bĭ laik -ðæt feloŭ ĭn ·ʃelĭ jŭ wə tɔkĭŋ ə:baut laas nait \—ə juwþ wĭð hɔrĭ hɛə.

skeitĭŋ.

:ðis ĭz ðə ·kouldĭst :dei wĭj v hæd ðis wintə: ·twelv dĭ:grijz əv frɔst ðis :mɔnĭŋ. d :juw :mijn twelv dĭ:grijz bĭ:lou ·ziərŏu? ^nou, twelv dĭ:grijz bĭ:lou ·frijzĭŋpoint \—twentĭ færĭnhəit \—twentĭ dĭ:grijz ^ə·bav :ziərŏu. :ou, əi fəgot; əi v :livd sŏu loŋ əbrɔd ðət əi fəgot :ɔl əbaut :færĭnhəit. əi dount wandə jŭ :got kənfjuwzd. əi wiʃ færĭnhəit wər əbolĭʃt; ·sentĭgreid z ðĭ ounlĭ ræʃənəl skeil \—ɔl saiən;tifĭk :men juwz ĭt. :wel \, ðər ə gud -menĭ ·aðə rĭ:fɔmz ðət l hæv tə -kam fəəst \—desĭməl koinĭdʒ \, :weits n meʒəz \, spelĭŋrĭfɔm \, ən lots əv aðəz. ʃuəlĭ ju douŋ gŏu in fə -ðæt pestĭlənt herĭsĭ ·spelĭŋrĭfɔm? :whai ĭt s simplĭ waipĭŋ aut ðə houl histrĭ ə ðə læŋgwĭdʒ. wel \, ðə fĭ·lolədʒĭsts \, hŭw ʃuəlĭ :ɔt tə nou best /, :sei ĭt :daz naþĭŋ ə ðə kaind: ĭn :fækt -ðei sei ðət wĭðaut spelĭŋrĭfɔm jŭ kaant -æv enĭ fĭlolədʒĭ ətɔl. wel, præps -ðɛə rait; ^ai :douŋ kɛə :matʃ əbaut ĭt′: əi v ðə konsə:leiʃən əv nouĭŋ ĭt wount -kam ĭn ᵛmai :taim. ðə best aagjəmənt əi evə həəd ə:genst spelĭŋrĭfɔm wəz :whot ·paipə :sed laas nait: hĭj :sed ĭf :pijpl wans bĭ:gin wĭð əbolĭʃĭŋ ðə preznt :sistĭm əv spelĭŋ, ðə nekst þĭŋ l :bij -ðei l :wont tŭ ə:bolĭʃ ðə :haus əv ^lɔdz. sŏu əi :sed ə gud þĭŋ tuw ĭf -ðei ·did\, whĭtʃ :sijmd tə ʃok ĭm greitlĭ.

d juw skeit? jes\, ə litl′; d juw? ᵛjes: əi m :raaðə fond əv ĭt\, :when əi kən :get gud ais′. əi sə:pouz ðə z ə ^gudijl əv :skeitĭŋ :gouz on ə:baut hiə\? jes\, -ðei :skeit ŏn ðə medŏuz; ðər ə dʒenrəlĭ ·fladz :aaftə krisməs. ʃə wĭ :gou ən -hæv ə luk ət ĭt? ^jes; ən :if ðĭ ais ĭz gud, wĭj kŋ kam bæk fər əuə skeits.

ĭz ĭt faa? ounlĭ ə:baut ə :mail n ə haaf′. əi kən hiə ðə riŋĭŋ ə ðə skeits ŏn ðĭ ais; əi laik tə :hiə -ðæt :saund: ĭt rĭmaindz mĭj əv :when əi wəz ə boi. əi :nevə ^kɛəd -matʃ fə skeitĭŋ :when əi wəz ə boi′; əi :laikt ·slaidĭŋ :betə; əi juws tə kən:sidə skeitĭŋ ə prĭtenʃəs ən ærĭstə;krætĭk pə:sjuwt\, ɔl -verĭ wel fə :groun ap :pijpl, bət not ðə þiŋ fə ·boiz. jes\, əi rĭmembə jŏ :teikĭŋ mĭj :aut fər ə slaid ŏn ə pond wĭð reilĭŋz :raund ĭt\, :when wĭj wər ɔl steiĭŋ ət jŏə haus -ðæt haad wintə. :ai wəz eit, ən juw wər ə:baut ten\, əi sə:pouz. ənd əi rĭ:membər əi þɔt jŭ ə verĭ :fain felŏu\, gouĭŋ :daun ə ·þəətĭ ŏ ·fɔtĭ :fijt slaid\, folŏud bəi ə misĭ·leinjəs ræbl əv skuwlboiz, butʃəboiz, potboiz, ənd erənboiz əv ɔl -sɔts\, wĭð ən ə:keiʒənəl pəlijsmən ŏ souldʒə: ĭt səətnlĭ kud nt bĭ :kɔld ən əristə;krætĭk ə:mjuwzmənt. əi rĭ:membə wĭj -hæd ðə mĭsfɔtʃən tə trip -ap ə butʃəboi\—ə big laut əv ə:baut ·siks·tijn\—ŏ :raaðər əi bĭ:lijv ·juw dĭd ĭt ŏn pəəpəs; ənd ĭj ·wei·leid əs ŏn əuə :wei houm, ən kræmd ə :lot əv ·snou :daun əuə neks. ðæt butʃəboi wəz ə :regjələ ·bæd n; d juw :nou -whot bĭkeim əv ĭm? nou ˋ, whot ˋ? hĭj :went əut tŭ əmerĭkə, ən wəz hæŋd fə hɔsstijlĭŋ.

whot ə ·kraud! ən luk əu -ðei v kat :ap ðĭ ais! əi douŋ :kɔl -ðæt skeitĭŋ: ĭt s :mɔə ləik stægərĭŋ -ouvər ə plaud fijld. tuw -menĭ boiz :tuw; əi dount laik boiz ŏn ðĭ ais: -ðɛər ɔlwĭz getĭŋ bĭ:twijn jŏ legz ən þrouĭŋ jŭ daun; əi laik ·leidĭz betə ˋ— -ðɛə kwaiətə. wel, ðər ə :gud -menĭ leidĭz ^tuw; ðeə z :misĭz ·neigl. whɛə ˋ? dount jŭ :sij -ðæt staut :fijmeil ĭn ðə tʃɛə? :whot, wĭ ðæt :jaŋ felŏu puʃĭŋ ĭt bĭhaind? jes; fainlukĭŋ wumən, iz nt ʃĭ ˋ? jes ˋ, bət :raaðə kɔs ´; ai prĭ:fəə :samþĭŋ ə litl :mɔr ĭjþiərĭəl; huw z ðə :jaŋ :felŏu ðət s prŏpelĭŋ -əə ˋ? :ðæt s jaŋ ·læm; hĭj z :wan ə ðə maastəz ĭn kobĭts skuwl. ðɛə z kobĭt ĭmself ˋ— -ðæt bĭnevələntlukĭŋ pætrĭaak wɔkĭŋ ŏn ðə bæŋk :bai ðŏuz wilŏuz. :ðɛə z ·neigl :tuw ˋ—dʒest :hævĭŋ ĭz ·skeits :put on. ĭz ðæt ðə mæn ðət ·bædʒə :sez luks ləik ə kombĭ:neiʃən əv ·aatʃ ·biʃəp, ·batlə, ən ·mauntĭbæŋk? əi :nevə həəd -ðæt, bət əi kən kwait :fænsĭ bædʒə seiĭŋ ĭt; ðə səətnlĭ ĭz ə :grein əv truwþ ĭn ĭt ˋ, ðŏu əv kɔs ĭt s grous ĭgzædʒə·reiʃən; bət əi m ʃuər ĭt s :ounlĭ ĭz mænə ˋ—əi :mijn ·neigl əv :kɔs: ðə z naþĭŋ ə ðə ·mauntĭbæŋk ə:baut neigl; hĭj z ə þarəlĭ gud felŏu ˋ—əz gud ə felŏu əz evə brijðd ˋ, ənd ə ·klevə :felŏu :tuw. bət əi :þɔt -ðei kɔld ĭm prə:fesə ·hambag. :ðæt -keim ə:baut ĭn ðĭs -wei. :when :neigl fəəst -keim :ouvə tŭ iŋglənd, hĭj :juws tə gĭv mjuwzĭklesns ət eitĭjnpens ən auə ˋ—hĭj wəz :raaðə :haad ap, -puə :felou. əz ĭj wəz ə ·forĭnə, :evrĭbodĭ :þɔt ĭj mas bĭj ə ·dʒəəmən ˋ, bĭ:koz ðə dʒəəmənz ə -satʃ ə ·mjuwzĭkl :pijpl; ənd əz ĭj :wɔ spektĭklz, -ðei :sed ĭj mas bĭj ə prə·fesə ˋ, ən :sou -ðei tŭk tə kɔlĭŋ ĭm prə·fesə. wan dei ə :litl gəəl aast ĭm whot ĭj wəz prə·fesər ŏv. sŏu ĭj :sed prə:fesər əv hambag ˋ—ŏ hombog ˋ, əz hij prənaunst ĭt. ðæt s əu ĭj gŏt ðə nikneim əv prə:fesə hambag. hĭj :tuk ĭt kwait gud·neitʃədlĭ, ənd :ijvn dʒoind ĭn ðə tʃaaf ə-genst ĭmself. :aaftə :ðæt ĭj bĭ-keim :verĭ popjələ ˎ, tĭl ət laast ĭj gŏt ðə maastəʃĭp əv modən læŋgwĭdʒĭz ĭn kobĭts skuwl. ·iz ĭj ə dʒəəmən? ^nou, ĭj ·spijks dʒəəmən ləik ə neitĭv, bət ðə ·dʒəəmənz :sei ĭj spijks ĭt wĭð ə forĭn :æksent. hĭj :spijks ·raʃən :tuw kwait fluəntlĭ; bət ðə ·raʃənz :sei ĭj :spijks ĭt wĭð ə :slait ·dʒəəmən :æksĭnt. hĭj :spijks ·poulĭʃ :tuw ˎ—sŏu oltə·geðə -wan daz nt ĭg:zæktlĭ :nou whot tə :meik əv ĭm. ᵛai bĭ:lijv ĭj z əv ə poulĭʃ ·dʒuw :fæmĭlĭ :setld ĭn ðə boltĭk provĭnsĭz əv raʃə.

ðæt boi skeits :raaðə wel: hĭj z ·æktʃŭəlĭ :duwĭŋ ə þrij bækwədz! əi nevə :sɔ ə boi :duw ·ðæt bĭ:fɔə. hĭj z not :duwĭŋ ĭt :kwait ·klijn ðŏu: hĭj ·skreips. ðɛər ĭj z daun! əi ᵛþɔt sŏu. əbzəəv ðə dignĭtĭ wĭð :whitʃ ĭj raizĭz ˎ, ən braʃĭz ðə nijz əv ĭz trauzəz ˎ, ən :hau tendəlĭ ĭj smuwðz ĭz pot hæt. :ðæt s :wan əv kobĭts :boiz: -ðɛər ɔl ləik ðæt ˎ— -ðei ɔl -æv ðə mænəz əv groun -ap :men ə ðə wəəld. ĭz :ðæt ðə rĭ:zalt ə ðə treinĭŋ -ðei -get ĭn ðə skuwl? səətnlĭ; ðə :prinsəpl -ðei gou ŏn :iz ðət ðə :biznĭs əv edʒŭ·keiʃən :iz tə prĭpɛə :boiz fə ðə :wəək əv laif ˎ—tŭ ĭnʃuə ðəm səksesfl kəriəz. əz kobĭt ən neigl :sei, ðĭ ouldfæʃənd dʒon bul əidiəl əv onĭst rafnĭs ən mænlĭ streit·fɔwədnĭs wount :duw nauədeiz: dĭ·plouməsĭ ən vəəsə;tilĭtĭ z whŏt s wontĭd; giv ə :boi ðə :treinĭŋ əv ə polĭʃt dĭploumətĭst, ən ĭj z ·ʃuə tə -get on ĭn ðə :wəəld. sŏu -ðei :duw evrĭþĭŋ -ðei kæn tə giv ðə :boiz ·dʒentlmənlĭ ən ·polĭʃt mænəz. -ðei v leit dinə ˎ, ən ðə bigə :boiz ər ĭks:pektĭd tə ·dres fə :dinə. -ðei :giv praizĭz tə ðə :boiz ðət dres :best ˎ, ən -hæv ðə best mænəz. ðə boiz -æv ə verĭ :gud ·taim əv ĭt: lemə·neid ən ·keik hændĭd raund djŭərĭŋ lesns. ĭn :fækt ðə :jaŋ raasklz -get sou pæmpəd -ðei douŋ ^kɛə tə :gou houm: -ðei :təən -ap -ðɛə nouzĭz ət plein dʒoints ən rais pudĭŋz. wan :boi æktʃŭəlĭ ræn ə-wei frəm houm bæk tə skuwl ĭn ðə :midl ə ðə krisməs holĭdĭz ˎ, bĭ:koz ĭz maðə :geiv ĭm ə trijkl

·pudĭŋ fə :dinə ; hĭj :sed ĭt -meid ĭz blad :boil. əi houp -ðei dount nĭglekt ðə ·morəl treinĭŋ ə ðə boiz ′. ou :nou ‵, ·kobĭt sijz tə ðæt : hĭj z ɔlwĭz ĭmpresĭŋ ŏn ðəm ðə nĭsesĭtĭ əv kaltĭveitĭŋ ə hai morəl stændəd ‵, ən pəsjuwĭŋ ðə haiĭst eþĭkl əidiəlz ‵—ðæt iz, əz faar əz ĭz kənsistənt wĭð getiŋ on ĭn laif.

ðεəz :misĭz ·neigl ə:gen ‵, ən :jaŋ ·who d jŭ :sei ĭz neim ĭz′ ? læm ‵—dadlĭ plæn·tædʒĭnĭt læm. hĭj :luks əz :if ĭj d -hæd ĭnaf əv ĭt. jes ‵, hĭj z not -verĭ fond əv :misĭz neigl ; ĭt s ·an;greitfl ŏv ĭm ðŏu ′ ; fə ʃij :got ĭm ðə pleis. jes ‵, bædʒə :sez ʃĭj bousts əv ĭt oupnlĭ ə:maŋ -əə frendz ‵—ʃĭj gouz əbaut seiĭŋ ' læm z ᵛmai boi ′.' not -verĭ pleznt fə ^him. nou ‵, ĭj daz nt laik ĭt ətɔl ; hĭj :sez fijmeil inflŭəns ĭz ðə fainĭst þĭŋ ĭn ðə wəəld :when ĭt s eksəsəizd ĭn ĭts lĭdʒitĭmĭt sfiə ‵— :ðæt :iz, ĭn fæmĭlĭ laif ; bət ðə z naþĭŋ :məə mistʃĭvəs ðən ·andəhænd fijmeil inflŭəns ĭn þiŋz -ðei nŏu :naþĭŋ əbaut. ·hæʒ ʃĭ sŏu :matʃ inflŭəns ĭn ðə :skuwl ? jes ‵, ʃĭj z got neigl kəmplijtlĭ :andər -əə þam ‵, ən kobĭt tuw. -həə ·greit əidiə(r) :iz ðət ɔl ðə maastəz ʃəd :bij əv dʒentl blad ‵, əz :ʃij kɔlz ĭt. :iʒ ʃĭ sŏu veri ærĭstə·krætĭk əəself -ðen ? ʃĭj :səətnlĭ ᵛþiŋks ʃĭj :iz ; hæv nt jŭ :həəd -əə tɔk əv :mai graandaŋkl :səə ritʃəd ? nou ‵, əi nevə -hæd ðə :pleʒər əv mijtĭŋ -əə ; ·huw wəz ðĭs -səə ritʃəd ‵ ? hĭj wəz lɔd mεər əv landən ‵, ŏ samþĭŋ ĭn ðə ·sitĭ əi bĭ:lijv. jŭw dount :sijm tə laik -əə :matʃ ^jŏself. nou ‵, əi dount ; ʃĭj -æz ə verĭ :bæd inflŭəns ŏn neigl ən kobĭt ‵, ən ðə kaunsl dʒenrəlĭ ; ĭt wəz ɔl þrŭw həə ðət puə bædʒəz əpointmənt wəz kænsld ət ðə laas moumĭnt. jes ‵, bædʒə :tould mĭj ɔl əbaut ĭt. hĭj -sed ðət when ðĭ əfεə wəz setld, neigl :keim ap tŭ ĭm wĭð ə þĭjætrĭkəl εə, ən :sed ' bij :not dĭshaatnd ‵, məi frend ; ·ai əv -dan evrĭþĭŋ əi kud :fə jŭ ; bət ðə godz ðəmselvz fait ĭn vein ə-genst ædvəəs destĭnĭ.' :bædʒə aaftəwədz :həəd frəm ə mæn ŏn ðə kaunsl ðət neigl sŏu faa frəm bækĭŋ ĭm, ə·pouzd ĭz əpointmənt ‵, ənd ·wɔnd ðəm ə:genst ĭm. ðə ·best ə ðə dʒouk woz ðət bædʒə wəz sou ʃuər ə ðə :pleis ðət ĭj lɔt ə dres kout n ə pot hæt ən haafədazn whait taiz \—ən nau -ðɛə nou ·juws tŭ ĭm, ĭj :sez. hĭj ɔt tŭ əv sent :in ðə bil tə :misĭz neigl. əi :dɛəsei ĭj wud \, :ounlĭ ĭj :þɔt ·neigl wəz ət ðə botəm əv ĭt; hĭj :sez ĭt s :ɔl hambag əbəut ĭz :bijĭŋ -andə misĭz :neiglz þam; hĭj :sez ĭt s ə miə ·dodʒ əv neiglz tə ʃift ðə rĭsponsə·bilĭtĭ :on tə :samwan els. hĭj tould mĭ ə·naðə kjuərĭəs :þiŋ. ĭt :sijmz -ðei :wans ĭkspeld ə :boi \—. -ðei ·nevər ĭkspel :boiz: -ðei -get rid ə ðəm kwaiətlĭ. wel \, :when -ðei -got ·rid əv ə :boi kwaiətlĭ ə litl whəil əgou /—əi þiŋk ĭt wəz bĭ:kos ĭj wud nt wɛər ə pot hæt /—ðə boi sed ðət neigl wəz ɔfl-ĭ kaind tŭ ĭm sam wijks bĭfɔə -ðei rout tŭ ĭz faaðər ə:baut ĭt: hĭj juws tə giv ĭm ·tʃokəlĭtkrijmz \, :ðou bĭfɔə :ðæt ĭj nevə :tuk enĭ pətikjələ ·noutĭs ŏv ĭm \—hĭj ijvn :juws tə wɔk əbəut ðə pleigraund wĭð ĭz aamz :raund ðə boiz nek. ðə :mous kjuəriəs þĭŋ :woz ðət ðis boi sed ðət -sam ə ðĭ ouldə :boiz, :when -ðei sɔ ðĭs, -ðei laaft \, ən tould ĭm tə luk aut fə ·skwɔlz: -ðei :sed ðət bitər ĭkspiərĭəns əd tɔt ðəm tə dĭs·trast neiglz frenʃĭp. :ai ʃəd ədvaiʒ jŭ not tə :pei ðə smɔlĭst ətenʃən tŭ :enĭþĭŋ bædʒə :sez ə:baut neigl: hĭj z ɔlwĭz sniərĭŋ -æt ĭm \, ən :meikĭŋ ĭnsinjŭ·eiʃənz ə:genst ĭm. ðə :fækt :iz, bædʒəz nætʃərəlĭ ən ilkəndiʃənd kæn·tæŋkərəs felŏu \, ən þrŭw wont əv tækt ən komən sens ĭz kəriə z bĭjn :raaðər ə feiljə ŏn ðə :houl \, ənd əv :kɔs :ðæt s :meid ĭm wəəs \, bĭsaidz -hævĭŋ ðĭs pəəsnl gradʒ ə:genst neigl \, whĭtʃ ᵛai bĭlijv z ɔl ĭmædʒĭ·neiʃən. əi mas kənfes əi :raaðə ·simpəþəiz wĭð :bædʒə; ənd ĭj sijmz tə :mij ə veri :gud felou \—:þarəlĭ onĭst ən streit·fɔwəd. :ou, ĭj z ᵛonĭst i:naf: hĭj z :raaðə ^tuw :onĭst \—hĭj z ɔlwĭz tokĭŋ əbəut onĭstĭ \, əz :if hij wə ðĭ ounlĭ :onĭst mæn ĭn ðə wəəld. ə:kodĭŋ tə him, evrĭ :mæn ŭw :gets on ĭn ðə :wəəld bəi tækt ən komən sens ən not tredĭŋ ŏn ðə touz əv men ĭn pauə z þarəlĭ dĭzonĭst \—ðæt s ĭz feivərĭt freiz. dʒest əz ·jɔə :feivrĭt freiz ĭz þarəlĭ :gud felŏu : ə:kɔdĭŋ tə juw, ·evrĭwanz ə þarəlĭ :gud felŏu '—ən :ðen jŭ gŏu ən tel mĭj ə :lot ə þiŋz əbəut ðəm tə ʃou ðət -ðɛər ĭgzæktlĭ ðĭ opəzĭt.

·hal·lou, :ðɛə z ənaðə :skuwl :kamĭŋ ŏn ðĭ ais '--pleiĭŋ ·hokĭ tuw ; əi wandə -ðei əlau -ðæt. kobĭts :boiz ə :gouĭŋ ɔf :nau : ðə hokĭ z tuw ·matʃ fə ðəm ; bĭ:saidz -ðei v :got tə dres fə dinə. əi :þiŋk ·wij d :betə :gou ən :duw ðə seim. əi :þɔt jŭ ·nevə drest fə dinə. əi put :on ə klijn kolə ', ðæt s ·mai əi:diə əv dresĭŋ fə dinə.

THE END.